mountain bike
MAINTENANCE

mountain bike
MAINTENANCE

FALCONGUIDE®

GUILFORD, CONNECTICUT
HELENA, MONTANA

AN IMPRINT OF THE GLOBE PEQUOT PRESS

GUY ANDREWS
Foreword by Gary Fisher

First published in Great Britain
by A&C Black Publishers Ltd
38 Soho Square, London W1D 3HB
www.acblack.com

Published in the United States
by The Globe Pequot Press
P.O. Box 480
Guilford, Connecticut 06437
United States of America
www.globepequot.com

All photographs © Gerard Brown
Cover and inside design by Lilla Nwenu-Msimang

Library of Congress Cataloging-in-Publication Data is available.
ISBN 0-7627-4088-4

Printed in China
First Edition/First Printing

CONTENTS

ACKNOWLEDGMENTS

My sincere thanks go to:

Everyone who helped supply equipment and help us on the photo shoots, namely: Caroline Griffiths at Madison for Shimano, Park Tools and a whole pile of other stuff; Brian Buckle at Trek for Gary Fisher, Klein and Trek bikes; Ross at ATB sales for Marin Bicycles; Ben and Russell at Kona Bicycles; Dom Mason and the 'gang' at DMR for bikes and components; Jamie Newall for riding all day for us and cleaning the bike too!; Alan Gunner at Fishers for SRAM; Shelley Childs at Cambrian for Continental Tires; Darren Mabbott from Silverfish for Race Face and Rock 'n' Roll lubes; Cedric Chicken of Chicken & Sons for Mavic, Sapim and Time components; Vince and Jim from Jim Walker and Co. for BRIKO; Stuart Mcghee from Evans cycles in Wandsworth; and Eden Imaging Studio.

Thanks also to Steve Goodwin, Alex Gates, Halina Simpson, Derek Manley and Keith Barton, all from Aylesbury Training Group. If you want to learn more about being a bike mechanic, their Park Tool School is an excellent way into the trade in the UK. These courses are superbly run by the ATG team. For more information, visit www.atg-cyclemechanics.co.uk.

Special thanks to Gerard Brown – without his patience, experience and attention to detail this book wouldn't have been as well illustrated – also to Alan Muldoon from MBR magazine for his extra insight and to Claire Dunn for making sense of it all.

Lastly, you don't know where you get your mechanical skills from but I'd especially like to pick out Frank Hornby, the man who invented Meccano, and my Dad, Keith Andrews – who taught me the benefits of both reading and ignoring the instruction manuals . . .

FOREWORD

Mountain biking: why do we do it?

We are away from the Cops, the Cars and the Concrete.
We dip in to the Endorphin pool.
We have uninterrupted time with our Buds.
We get way out in the woods ripping and tearing, air time, riding the natural rollercoaster
to quiet places we have never been.

This is how it is and how it's always been. It's about self-sufficiency, your own power and
your machine. Learn more about them and you are a free bird.

In the old days you would start a ride with six riders and three would finish walking with
broken parts in their hands. The bikes weighed around 50 lbs – we called them Klunkers.
The gears ground, grated and hated you, the brakes squealed and you had to stop on the
downhills and wave your hands around to stop the numbness. Parts that were never
intended for this use/abuse would crack and come flying apart. We were in the middle of
nowhere – ride Pine Mountain and you might see a hiker or maybe no one all day. When one
of us broke down our attitude was 'We have all day to fix it' or 'Do you want to walk out?'.
The creative repair ruled: stuffing grass into a flat tire after the last inner tube was used or
using the baling wire from a California rural fence or forming a fix with Manzenita tree limbs
with the use of the Klunker multitool, a pair of vise grips.

That was 30 years ago. Since then, The Klunker has transformed into The Mountain
Bike and thousands of creative minds have pored over every detail. The new bikes almost
float up the climbs, the feeling of flying comes often, full suspension really works for the
rider and at the end of the day you will be riding your bike better on 99 out of 100 rides if
you know what you are doing.

That's what this book is all about: what to look for on a day-to-day basis, the preparation and upkeep that keeps the ride sweet. Guy Andrews cuts to the chase, with his real-
world experience and intimate knowledge of the bits and pieces and how and where they
play. Guy advises how and when to fix it and when it's advisable to seek help and go to your
local wrench.

The knowledge in this book is the stuff that makes today's bikes work like they should.
It is the stuff you wish came in the owner's manual instead of the legalese that a maker is
obliged to include. Every mountain bike needs this book, for it will be the happier and so
will you.

Gary Fisher

1

Introduction

The mountain bike is the result of some clever sideways thinking by a bunch of American cyclists in the mid-1970s, who took some cruiser-style bikes to the top of a California mountain and raced them down a narrow off-road trail. They called these crudely customised bikes 'clunkers', but these pioneers had really started something. They realized you could reach some stunning scenery and terrain, if your bike was up to it. You could even cover great distances, riding over mountains too, if the bike had extra gears. It wasn't an invention as such – more a development of bicycle technology – but before too long the mountain bike was born.

THE MOUNTAIN BIKE

Modern mountain bikes are very tough. They can take you anywhere: to date they have been ridden across polar ice caps, through jungles and deserts and even across the biggest mountains. This tough efficiency appeals to everyone – even bike couriers and commuters choose mountain bikes for their ability to pound the pot-holed city streets without complaint.

Mountain bikes are constantly evolving. Nowadays, they have 27 gears, suspension and disc brakes and have come a long way from the single-geared 'clunkers' of the 1970s. Frames are now made from heat-treated aluminum, titanium and carbon fiber rather than just traditional steel. And the manufacturers are constantly updating components to make them stronger and lighter.

Over time, changes in riding styles have meant that mountain bikes now come in a variety of different guises: cross-country hardtail, full suspension trail bike, full suspension downhill racing rig, jump bike, trials bike, single-speed, commuter – the list goes on.

But mountain bikes do go wrong. No matter how tough they are, eventually the components may fail, wear out or break. So this easy-to-follow, step-by-step guide to fixing your mountain bike will help to keep you riding. We'll take you from the basic checkups through to advanced repairs and trailside fixes. However, seeing as prevention is always better than cure, we'll also show you how to keep your bike clean, well adjusted and free from trouble.

Types of mountain bike

Trail bike

The mountain bike was originally designed to go any-where and this is the basic premise of the modern-day trail bike. Designed to be comfortable, it also has to be serviceable – there is no point having stuff on the bike you cannot easily fix with simple tools. Lockout for the suspension is popular, as is adjustable travel to suit different terrains and riding styles. You can carry a hardtail (a bike with a rigid rear triangle – no suspension on the rear wheel) up hills easily, but a full suspension bike can be more fun downhill and far more comfortable when riding off-road all day.

Variations on the trail bike include the freeride bike, which has more travel and a beefier frame and is therefore more suitable for extreme trails. A hardtail can also be beefed up for this type of riding, using forks with 100 mm travel (with corrected geometry to allow for the extra travel) and reinforced 'gusseted' frames. Full suspension bikes for this type of riding have up to 150 mm of travel front and rear.

Cross-country race bike

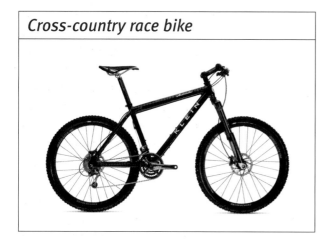

Racing mountain bikes are usually light and fast first and comfortable second and are usually made from lightweight aluminum, carbon fiber or titanium. They have shorter travel forks (80–100 mm), which are usually air sprung and have a lockout option for climbing. Some racers do use full suspension bikes if the course suits it, but most prefer the reliable and lightweight hardtail option. Racing mountain bikes have higher gearing than trail bikes, and tubeless tires and disc brakes are becoming more common in this class.

Variations on the cross-country race bike include the freeride hardtail, which is used by people who ride hard but still want a bike that will cope with riding uphill. These bikes have a heavier build and longer travel for faster descending and big hits.

Full suspension DH (downhill) bike

This is the complete opposite of the cross-country race bike in that weight, although an issue, is not the top priority. Full suspension bikes have to be mechanically perfect – especially the suspension, which can be adjusted to suit different terrains and conditions and usually has six to eight inches of front and rear travel. Most of the top riders have a full-time mechanic to look after their 'rig'. Personal choice has a big influence on bike setup, and no two bikes or riders will be the same. Some riders run fatter tires of up to 2.5 inches at lower pressures for increased traction. The brakes on down-hill bikes have bigger disc rotors and more powerful calipers, which give more stopping power. Downhill bikes also need fewer gears and use chain retainers to prevent the chains jumping off when the bike hits bumps at speed. 'Triple-clamp' motorbike-style forks can also be clamped to the bike at the top and bottom of the head tube for extra strength.

Variations on the full suspension DH bike include the Four Cross or dual race bike. A Four Cross event is like a downhill BMX race, with riders using something resembling a freeride hardtail or a jump bike; if the course is rocky, sometimes a short-travel suspension bike will be preferred. Tighter geometry and lighter wheels add faster accelera-tion for getting out of the start gate first.

Jump bike

Like full suspension DH bikes, jump bikes have to be mechanically bomb proof. This type of bike is strongly influenced by BMX bikes, partly because they need to be exceptionally maneuverable and also because they need to be super-strong. Often, riders will ride a sin-glespeed for reliability and strength, which also means there is less to go wrong after a crash. Suspension is long travel (over 100 mm) and very burly. Frames are made from high-tensile cromoly steel or heat-treated aluminum.

Variations on the jump bike include the trials bike, which doesn't really fit into any of these categories but is as simple as a jump bike. Trials bikes have wide handlebars for increased control, sharp, powerful brakes for stopping dead and hopping onto obstacles, singlespeed, and rigid forks.

Commuter bike

This mountain bike design is perfect for the city streets. Commuter bikes are usually steel or aluminum hardtails fitted with slick, narrow road tires. Gears are on the higher side with closer road ratios on the cassette and larger chainrings than cross-country bikes. Some have suspension forks, but these aren't always necessary, and the simplicity of a set of rigid forks and low-maintenance components is a major advantage for a bike that is used day in, day out. Fitting wider tires makes these bikes suitable for riding on bike paths and railtrails and many riders use the same bike for on- and off-road riding, swapping the wheels over for hitting the dirt at the weekends.

Variations on the commuter bike include adventure and touring-style bikes. Mountain bikes offer great load-carrying capabilities, have easily serviceable parts and plenty of options for carrying luggage – just add a set of slicks and a rack to your mountain bike and you can explore the world.

Singlespeed bike

The singlespeed is a reaction to the over-hyped mountain bike industry, and is perfect for when you really can't stand adjusting your gears any more. Singlespeeds can be used for cross-country riding or as a jump bike, are great in muddy conditions and can be made up out of old frames and parts. Many people prefer the pure riding experience that comes with a simple bike – and who can argue with that?

Singlespeed bikes are growing in popularity and all sorts of riders are now using them for different mountain bike activities: jumping, trials, dual descending races and just for riding to work. After all the years of development it is still the 'riding' part of mountain biking rather than the technology that is the most enjoyable, and singlespeeding sums up this powerful philosophy pretty well.

Other bikes

Cyclo-cross bike

OK, it's not a mountain bike, but it is a significant fore-runner to the mountain bike. Basically a road bike with road-sized wheels and big clearances for mud, cyclo-cross bikes also have relaxed seat and head angles and high bottom brackets, which sets them apart from road race bikes. However, they do still have cantilever brakes and rigid forks.

BMX

Another forerunner to the mountain bike, the BMX has a strong following among trail riders and jump riders who want to perfect their technique. Small, strong and simple, they are perfect for crashing, and good BMX riders make excellent mountain bikers.

Bike map

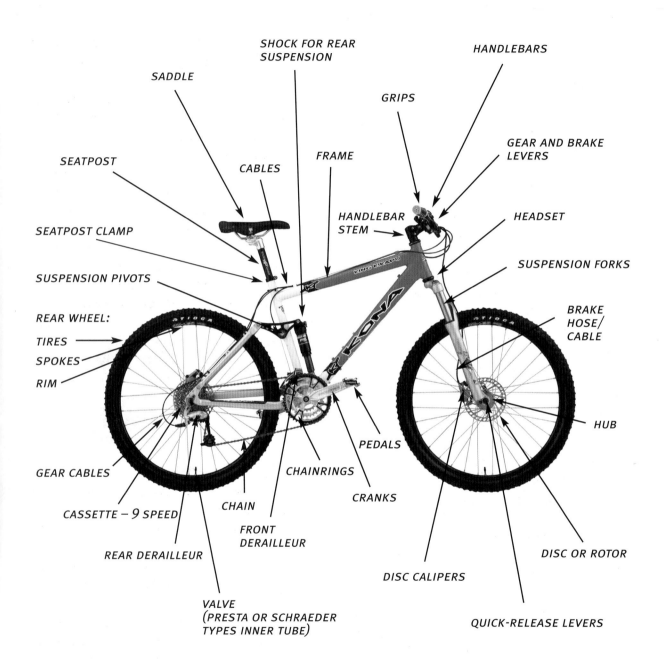

SHOCK FOR REAR SUSPENSION

HANDLEBARS

SADDLE

GRIPS

GEAR AND BRAKE LEVERS

SEATPOST

CABLES

FRAME

SEATPOST CLAMP

HANDLEBAR STEM

HEADSET

SUSPENSION PIVOTS

SUSPENSION FORKS

REAR WHEEL:

BRAKE HOSE/ CABLE

TIRES

SPOKES

RIM

GEAR CABLES

PEDALS

CHAINRINGS

HUB

CASSETTE – 9 SPEED

CHAIN

CRANKS

FRONT DERAILLEUR

REAR DERAILLEUR

DISC OR ROTOR

DISC CALIPERS

VALVE (PRESTA OR SCHRAEDER TYPES INNER TUBE)

QUICK-RELEASE LEVERS

Buying a bike

A while ago I was handed a $130 'mountain bike' to build from a box. It was the bargain type from a large high-street retailer, who wanted to see if I could show them how to prepare the bike to meet the relevant standards. Three hours later I still hadn't finished – there was so much wrong with the manufacture of the bike that I just couldn't make it safe. Eventually, it worked well enough to ride up and down the street, but the minute this thing hit the dirt it would fall apart like a clown car at the circus. The message here is: you get what you pay for.

With a quality bike from a *recognized* mountain bike manufacturer, the assembly process would have taken about an hour, such is the quality of instructions and parts from a decent factory. A 'true' mountain bike will come with full instructions for the consumer, details of any special parts (Shimano usually supplies instructions, and suspension forks normally have their own special instructions too), a PDI (Pre-Delivery Inspection) check list and, lastly, a warranty card. Any bike that can't supply this information should be avoided. Mountain biking is very hard on your bike and, when your life can depend on the quality and function of the equipment, you need to know you have done everything possible to prevent failure. So, it's far better to use a bike that is up to the job in the first place. This also means a bike that has been professionally assembled and checked from new, which is why your first port of call should be a quality local dealer.

Historically speaking, the entry-level mountain bike has always cost around $650–900. Because this is a very competitive price point these bikes are often very good value, featuring quality parts and a well-made frame. However, entry-level bikes are not designed and built to be pushed to the limits, so as your riding improves you will probably want to upgrade what you ride.

Remember that your main priorities are the frame, then the suspension forks, then the wheels, then the contact points (saddle, handlebars and pedals) and, lastly, the components. Components are last on the list because they will wear out in time and, should you want to upgrade them, you can do it when they wear out. The frame, suspension forks and wheels are always the most expensive parts of a bike, so look for the manufacturers that put the most effort into these areas and don't be fooled just because the bike has an XT rear derailleur or the added attraction of (poor-quality) disc brakes.

Look for the details, as sometimes corners are cut to save money – usually where you can't see it, for example the chain or the bottom bracket where the manufacturer may use a Shimano XT or LX chainset and a much cheaper bottom bracket. Likewise, chains can be cheaper than the rest of the drivetrain parts and, as the chain is the important moving part, it's better to have a good one.

Most current Shimano and SRAM mountain bike components are designed specifically for riding off-road. Always beware of gear components that you haven't heard of, as they may well just not be a match in quality for the job. Also, in my experience it's better to keep to one gear brand throughout; this way you will be less likely to have any issues with warranty or incompatibility.

Tips for buying a bike

As with most things in life, there will be good and bad points about your new bike, but here are a few tips you should always consider before buying a new bike.

1. Take an experienced mountain biking friend with you to give you advice. Research the brands you like the look of. Phone the manufacturers for catalogs and take a balanced view, and use the internet – www.bikemagic.com and www.mtb-review.com both have massive user review sections, which can provide interesting insights.

2. Buy a range of up-to-date magazines to consider your options. Find back issues of group tests of bikes in your price range, or even e-mail the magazine to ask their opinion.

3. Find out each manufacturer's best sellers.

4. Ask these questions at each shop you visit:
   - What size do I need and, if you haven't got one in that size, can you order it in? (See opposite for more information on sizing.)
   - Can I have a test ride? (See page 9 for more information on test rides.)
   - Do you provide a free first service?
   - Within reason, can I swap parts (saddle, stem, handlebars and so on) to get the exact fit I want?

The answer to all of these questions should be yes.

5. Consider that you will need after-sales support, so you'll need to build loyalty with the shop. Don't just buy more cheaply elsewhere and then expect a local dealer to fix or deal with the warranty on your new bike for free. It's always worth thinking about buying some extras (helmet, gloves, tools and so on) when you are at the shop buying your bike. This is probably the most you will spend in the shop at one time, so they may well offer you a few incentives even if it's just a free bottle and an inner tube.

6. Don't be lured by discounted bikes, special offers or ex-demonstration bikes unless you are absolutely sure it's the bike for you and it's the right size.

7. If the shop doesn't have your size, wait until they can get one. It's better to leave it a little longer and have the right bike.

8. Always ask local mountain bikers for recommendations and ask them about the local shops, for example which one is good for advice and which one specializes

in particular brands, as it's always better to go to a dealer who has a good reputation. Ask lots of questions in the shop and make sure they have a good mechanic and a well-equipped (preferably tidy) workshop. They should also offer you a free first service and warranty back-up.

Sizing

Most reputable bike dealers will be able to help you with picking the right size bike. As with most large purchases it's worth getting a few opinions. For the standard cross-country riding position you are looking for comfort first and foremost, so feeling relaxed and being able to move freely are essential.

The following is only a guide and, as everybody is different, please make sure you seek personal advice from an experienced cycle fitter.

1. *Stand-over height* – the distance between the top tube and the floor – needs to be lower than your inside leg measurement so, should you have to step off the bike in a hurry, you won't have a nasty shock as your crotch smacks onto double-butted aluminum (ouch). You need about 2–3 inches minimum.

2. *Reach* – the distance between the handlebars and the saddle – is very important on a mountain bike. Your arms should be comfortably bent and the saddle-to-bar drop should allow you to sit with a relatively straight back. A shorter handlebar stem will quicken the steering and improve control, but being too cramped can prevent you from shifting your weight across the saddle.

3. Correct *saddle height* is interpreted in a variety of ways. The general consensus is that your leg should be slightly bent at the bottom of the pedal stroke, without your hips having to sway on the saddle to perform the stroke. But this is open to interpretation, so have an experienced fitter check your saddle height.

4. Much of *bike-fit fine-tuning* can be done by exchanging components such as the saddle and stem. Test ride the bike after each change and make sure you are happy with the setup before you leave the shop.

Women's fit

Women's bikes are designed specifically to suit a female rider. In general terms, women tend to have a shorter body and longer legs than men. This means that a long top tube will have to be countered with an upright seatpost and a shorter stem. It is even better to have a shorter top tube too, which is why there are so many brands that have a specific women's bike in their range. Women's saddles are wider to offer more support and handlebars can be narrower to account for narrower shoulders. Again, spend time with the shop staff and get the bike comfortable – ensure you are happy before you leave the shop.

The test ride

You may have to leave your credit card (or your car keys, other half, friend, dog) as security in the shop before they will let you out on a test ride. When you leave the shop, relax and take the bike for a gentle spin. Stop somewhere quiet and have a good look over what you are about to buy. If you aren't 100 percent happy, don't feel pressured to buy – try something else instead.

Self-build bikes

In time you may want to have a go at building your own bike. Frame-only deals can offer excellent value, but be aware that using second-hand or used parts can create problems as you build. Things like front derailleurs and seatposts often vary in size and, unless you have all the right tools, you can easily make an expensive mistake.

Second-hand bikes

Like self-build, buying a second-hand bike can be a bit of a lottery. You may think you have a bargain, but if the bike has had any serious crash damage it could be an expensive mistake. Ideally, you should only buy a bike that has had little or no use.

If the drivetrain and brakes show signs of wear, the chances are some parts of it are about to need replacing. If this is the case, you will need to factor it into the bidding process, or reconsider the purchase if it will cost you more than the bike is worth to replace the worn-out parts. This is where taking an experienced riding friend is invaluable, as they will be able to spot the tell-tale signs of misuse immediately.

As with all second-hand purchases, especially online, be careful not to give out any personal details to people unless you know who they are.

2

Tools

I have owned my fair share of bikes over the years and have collected a fairly comprehensive tool kit too. The bikes still come and go but my tools should last a lifetime. This is why you should always buy good-quality tools, as you will use them to fix lots of bikes. Specialist bike tools are expensive, but they make complicated procedures a breeze and will also ensure you don't damage your new components and your bike, or hurt yourself. Botching jobs with cheap tools only ends in compromise, and if you have a good-quality bike it deserves the tools to complement it.

THE HOME WORKSHOP

Home workshop tool kit

For a modest outlay you can cover most home workshop jobs. Frame tools, specialist tools and cutting tools do cost a fair amount, but in time you may consider them a worthwhile investment. In the meantime, the best advice is to buy components from a local shop and get their mechanic to fit them for you if you don't have the tools yourself. However, as you become a more competent mechanic you may want to consider how much you spend in the bike's workshop compared to how much the tools will cost you.

This is the basic set of home workshop tools that will cover most of your needs:

- Allen keys – 1.5, 2, 2.5, 3, 4, 5, 6, 8 and 10 mm are the sizes most often used
- floor pump
- chain cleaner
- cleaning brushes
- pliers (flat and needle nose)
- cable cutters
- screwdrivers (small and large; flat and Phillips-head)
- nylon hammer (or mallet) and ball-peen (metal-working) hammer
- a set of metric, open-ended wrenches from 6 mm to 24 mm
- cassette lock ring tool
- chain whip
- chain tool
- cable puller
- 'poker' sharp-ended tool like an awl
- star nut-setting tool
- adjustable wrench
- cone wrenches (17 mm, 15 mm and 13 mm)
- pedal wrench
- workshop quality chain tool

- chain checker (for measuring chain wear)
- torque wrenches
- crank-removing tool
- bottom bracket tools
- headset wrenches (optional)
- wheel-truing stand
- spoke wrenches

- You may also find the following items useful:
- disc brake bleed kit
- hacksaw (standard and junior)
- files (flat and half round)
- socket set

More advanced home tools

As you become more experienced, add the following items to your workshop tool kit:

- headset press
- headset cup remover
- crown race remover
- crown race setting tool
- rear derailleur hanger straightening tool
- set of taps for threads
- rear dropout alignment tools
- disc brake facing kit
- steerer cutting guide.

Advanced and professional workshop tools

- head tube reamer and facing kit
- bottom bracket tapping and facing kit
- fork crown facing kit
- seat tube reamer
- frame alignment tool
- chainline gauge
- wheel dishing stick
- spoke tension meter.

Out on the trail

Your basic kit should contain a folding set of Allen keys, a screwdriver, two tire levers, a tube or two and a set of emergency patches. A saddle pack will carry the basic kit so you won't have to fill your pockets with tools. For longer rides, you might want to add a chain tool, a spoke wrench, a small wrench and some minor spares, such as brake pads and chain links.

Your full kit for traveling farther afield should include:

- tire levers
- two spare tubes
- puncture kit or emergency patches
- tire boot
- spoke wrench and spare spoke (cable spokes are good for emergencies)
- a good pump that can double up as a shock pump (if you have air forks or rear suspension)
- a quality chain tool and a few spare links and pins
- Allen keys – usually 2.5, 3, 4, 5, 6 and 8 mm
- Leatherman-style multitool with pliers and a sharp knife
- small dropper bottle of chain oil
- zip ties
- spare cables and brake pads (only really essential if you are miles from a bike shop).

TRAIL TOOL TIPS

- Spokes can be taped to a frame tube or hidden in the seatpost.
- Cable spokes are handy for quick repairs and, as they hook into the spoke holes rather than having to be pushed through, you don't have to remove the cassette to repair it.
- Always leave your trail tool kit intact and keep it just for riding. Taking tools out to fix your bike at home will mean you'll leave your tire levers on the kitchen table and not have them with you when you really need them...
- Carry a spoke wrench on your key ring – this makes your keys easier to find too!
- Tool kits can be stuffed into old drink bottles and placed in a spare bottle cage. Make sure it can't rattle out by securing it with a toe strap.
- If you are riding with friends, there's no need to double up on shock and tire pumps. Spread the tools around so you're not all carrying the same stuff.

Hydration-type backpacks are ideal for carrying more kit, especially the bulky items like inner tubes and your shock pump. It's better to carry this stuff on your back, away from your bike but also away from your pockets, which can become saggy and annoying when you're hopping the bike over obstacles.

Workshop setup

A home workshop is a bit of a luxury, but fixing your bike in the kitchen is never a great idea. So here are some bike storage ideas and tips for setting up your workshop at home.

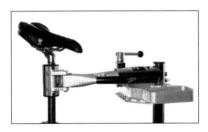

1. A stable work stand is essential. The best workshop type will be fixed to a wall or a solid workbench, so jobs that require bashing or heavy leaning won't make the stand move around the floor as you 'dance' with your bike.

2. Put down a mat for spillage. Remember that if you have to fix your bike in the kitchen, you will need something on the floor to soak up the mess. Workshop mats are readily available from bike or tool shops. They also keep your feet warm in the winter.

3. Hooks and lockable anchor points are a good idea, just in case you are broken into. Storing your bike(s) like this also prevents them from falling over and getting scratched by the lawn mower.

4. A solid workbench makes tough jobs like fitting headset parts or cutting down fork steerers easy. A tool board helps you find tools quickly, and quality tools should be stored in a tool box if your workshop is damp. You can also assemble a field tool box that you can take with you to races or trail rides so you can fix emergencies in the parking lot.

5. The vise needs to be properly bolted and secured to the solid workbench. A vise is essential for hub and headset jobs, and a pair of replaceable 'soft jaws' for the vise will help to protect valuable and sensitive components.

6. Your wheel jig should preferably be bench-mounted. A solid wheel jig makes truing wheels far easier. If you intend to learn how to build wheels, or just want to get better at home truing, then a wheel jig is a must-have item.

7. An electric drill will help with frame repairs and removing seized SPD bolts, and a bench-mounted grinder is useful for repairs and customizing components, but care must be taken when working to wear the right PPE (see Health and Safety warning on page 17).

8. Torque wrenches take the guesswork out of assembling airplanes, car engines and machines, and enable engineers to fasten bolts to manufacturers' recommended figures. This type is simple to use – set the level on the screw gauge on the handle

shown in Newton metres (Nm), then add the correct Allen or bolt head (they have either a $3/8$ inch or a $1/4$ inch socket drive) and tighten the bolt until the handle 'gives' with a click. This type is perfect for most Allen bolts on a bike.

9. Park Tools version of a torque wrench has a beam, which 'bends' when the handle is balanced, allowing you to read off the torque on the dial. You'll need a bigger one like this for cassette lock rings, cranks and bottom brackets. On mountain bikes it is critical to use recommended torque settings, for warranty reasons and for safety – especially on suspension forks and disc brakes with many moving parts and fastenings. All well-trained mechanics will use a torque wrench – don't build a bike up without one.

10. Mountain bike tires have a large volume and take a lot of air, so a floor pump will set tire pressures quickly and accurately and is far better than a mini pump. However, some pressure gauges are more reliable than others, so get a separate accurate tire-pressure gauge too.

11. You will develop preferences for particular brands of lubes and greases, but the modern bicycle requires a selection of advanced lubricants to keep it running sweetly:

· ti prep (or copper slip) – a grease with tiny copper flakes in it, which prevents titanium and alloys from seizing; this must be used on all titanium threads;
· anti-seize grease – this is for large threads and components that stay put for long periods (seatposts,
· bottom bracket threads, headset cups and pedal threads);
· PTFE (Teflon)-based light dry lube – this is preferred for summer use and assemblies like derailleurs and brake caliper pivots;
· heavy wet lube – this is best for wet weather as it's harder to wash away than dry lube;
· silicone greases – use these for intricate moving parts like pedal and hub bearings;
· waterproof greases – use these for components that get ignored for long periods like headset bearings;
· degreaser – used for cleaning moving parts and components that get covered with muck;
· bike wash – this speaks for itself; use it for tires, frame tubes and saddles;
· release agent – this is good for removing seized seatposts and stubborn bottom brackets. Be careful as it can ruin your paintwork, and your skin.

Workshop practices

Health and safety

Lubricants, disc-brake fluid, degreasers and bike washes look after your bike well enough, but they can ruin your skin – always read the instructions and labels on cans before you start work. Take care and use appropriate PPE (Personal Protective Equipment) when working on your bike. Latex gloves and aprons are a great idea and safety glasses are a must when using release agents or operating grinders and drills. Using the right tools helps too.

Disposal of hazardous substances

Hydraulic brake fluid and shock oils should be properly disposed of after use. Your local city dump will have a facility for dumping this stuff. DOT 4 and 5 brake fluids are very bad for the environment unless they are dealt with properly. Collect the waste in a container and find out where you can take it. Your local bike shop may also be able to dispose of it correctly for you.

Read the instructions

This may seem obvious, but it is very important. Warranties and guarantees are only any good if you install things correctly. Even the simplest of components will have some recommendations from the manufacturer – so stick to them. Use the recommended tools and torque settings. If in doubt, contact the shop or the manufacturer. Don't make expensive mistakes.

3

Basic bike setup

Once you have bought your bike, it will be properly prepared and checked over by the shop mechanic (pre-delivery inspection or PDI). The shop may ask you if you have any personal setup preferences, and they will also make sure that the gears are properly adjusted and the brakes are functioning safely. So, in theory your bike will be ready to take to the trails.

THE BASICS

However, there are some things you may want to adjust when you get the bike home, mainly to suit your personal position on the bike and the controls, which the mechanic will have adjusted to a 'nominal' position. The following steps are very basic adjustments, but they are the things you are most likely to want to change or put the finishing touches to once you have got your bike home.

Always ask the shop to run through anything on the bike you are unsure of and never touch anything that may require an experienced mechanic – or wait until you have read the rest of this book!

Tools required:
· **Allen keys**
· **torque wrench**

Brake lever angle

1 Inexperienced riders tend to place the levers flat to the handlebars, but the angle of the brake lever should be similar to the angle your arm takes to reach the handlebar; your wrists should be as straight and comfortable as possible when they are placed on the bars. This enables the tendons and muscles in your arm to pull in a linear motion, which is the most efficient way.

2 Adjusting the lever angle is simple. There is a 4 or 5 mm Allen bolt under the brake-lever clamp and, depending on the make of your bike, this can be accessed easily. The brake lever can also be swapped if you prefer the left to be the rear brake, for example. The lever can also be moved inward or outward on the bar. Get one lever precisely adjusted before you start on the other one to give you a reference point for how the lever was previously set.

3 The gear pod adjusting bolt is also here. You may have to depress the levers to get the Allen key into the socket. Bondhus Allen keys, which can be used at an angle, are a good idea for reaching awkward fixing bolts like these. The pods are designed to fit snugly to the brake lever, but be aware that the cable adjuster needs to be accessed easily – so don't rest it where you can't reach it.

Brake lever reach

1 Setting the lever reach is quite simple, but you do need to assess where your fingers will pull on the lever. Ideally, your first two fingers should be able to fold easily over the lever. As the lever is activated, the fingers shouldn't feel any strain as they pull the lever toward the bar. This may sound obvious now, but on a long descent brakes are essential and if your fingers cramp up or can't reach the levers it can be dangerous.

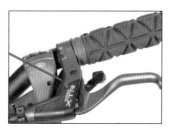

2 All cable-activated brake levers have a reach adjustment screw. So, if you have small hands, or want to get more purchase on the lever, look to experiment with this reach screw. Remember that screwing this lever in will also affect the cable length, so double check the brakes before you ride off. If you adjust it a great deal, be aware that the lever may hit the handlebars before the brakes activate. Experiment with cable adjustment too, as this can allow the brakes to have more or less feel at the lever.

3 Hydraulic disc brakes also have a reach adjustment screw. Depending on which system you are using, it is usually behind the lever on the plunger spigot. Only make small adjustments as this can affect the pull of the lever. For more on hydraulic disc brakes see pages 83–85.

4 In the 'full-on' braking position the fingers should close over the brake and lock the wheels up. Once you are happy that this is the case, check that the levers are symmetrical and tighten all the fixing bolts. The brake and gear levers need to be tight enough that they don't move under braking or shifting, but not so tight that they cannot be moved in the event of a stack.

Seatpost and saddle

1 The seatpost should be greased regularly, unless it is made out of carbon fiber. It's likely you will want to lower the seatpost out on the trail for long rocky descents and technical sections, which means you will need to be able to move the saddle quickly. A seatpost can seize very quickly if you neglect to regrease it regularly.

2 The saddle should be flat (line it up with a brick wall or use a spirit level to check this). If you feel the saddle needs to point downward, it is probably too high in relation to the handlebars. See pages 23–24 for more on saddle height and bike position.

3 Check that the seatpost quick release is tight in the frame, as it is possible for this to slip gradually over a long ride. The principle of this lever is the same as that of a wheel quick release. If you have trouble securing the seatpost (and you find you don't change your saddle height very often), change the collar for one that fastens with an Allen bolt as these can be more secure.

Releasing the V-brakes

1 Unhooking the V-brakes will allow you to remove the wheels. The brake calipers will fall apart to allow the fat tire to clear the pads. The secret is to squeeze the two brake arms firmly together so that the pads touch the rims. This can often be enough to slacken the cable and allow the noodle to fall out.

2 With your free hand grab the noodle and pull it sideways and away from the opposite caliper. This will pop the head of the noodle out of the retaining cage. Pull the cable through the slot in this cage. Don't wrench the cable out as it can damage the cable inner – you do need to be firm but don't jerk at the noodle.

3 When replacing the noodle, it is essential to make sure that the noodle head is placed securely into the retaining cage. It is possible for the noodle to snag on the edge of this cage and give the impression that it is inserted correctly, so always double check. Lastly, pull hard on the lever to check the action is perfect.

4 This is what the V-brake should look like when reassembled.

TIPS

If you are still having trouble, the brakes may need slackening off a little; you shouldn't have to struggle to unhook the brake. You can use the brake adjuster for this (set the brakes up so you can screw them in a little to provide the necessary slack in the cable) or undo the bolt on the caliper itself and let a little cable through. Before you return the noodle to the brake, slide it off the end of the cable and relubricate it. Use a wet lube or synthetic grease if you have some to hand. This part of the brake system is usually the part that provides the most friction as water and grime can build up unnoticed. See pages 69–88 for more on cable and brake setup.

Finding the right riding position

The wrong riding position can cause you all sorts of problems, in particular mountain bikers' bad back syndrome. Here are some suggestions to help you get it right; get a friend to help you, take photographs or use a full length mirror to help you get the best balanced position.

Saddle height

Too low

This will place excessive strain on the knees, but is popular with downhillers and trials riders as they need to get the saddle well out of harm's way. This is okay for short periods, but you should never ride for prolonged stretches like this.

Too high

This often creates back problems as the rider will have to stretch to reach the pedals at the bottom of each stroke, which tilts the pelvis and pulls on the lower back muscles. The same principle applies if you bob back and forth excessively when riding hard as your back will tire and start to hurt. This is often why back pain is especially bad after a hard hilly ride or race.

About right

The knee should be slightly bent at the bottom of the pedal stroke. An easy way to judge this is to have the heel of your foot on the pedal with your leg fully extended at the bottom of the stroke, then pedal backward. If you find that you rock from side to side excessively, your saddle is too high and you need to reset it so you feel smooth in this position. This way, when the ball of your foot is placed on the pedal there will be a bit of extra slack built in to your saddle height.

Note: This is only a guide – some riders will require more careful adjustments. If you alter your saddle height, do it by small increments of no more than 5 mm at a time and give yourself a few weeks to get used to it. That's why it's best to change position during the winter months as you won't be riding as regularly.

Stem fore/aft position

Too cramped

This will make you arch your back and stress the lower muscles. It also means you ride with your weight further forward, which will make the steering sluggish.

Too stretched

This usually forces you to lock out your arms and strain your neck to see ahead, both of which will contribute towards low back pain. The handling will feel sketchy and a bit too light.

About right

A balanced position means that you will be able to stretch out comfortably and bend your arms to assist in shock absorption. With the stem in the right position, your weight will be better distributed over the bike – if it is too short, the saddle will have to be pushed too far back; too long and the saddle will be too far forward.

Saddle fore/aft position

Too far back

This is good for climbing power and pedaling comfort over a long ride, but places extra strain on neck, arm and shoulder muscles.

Too far forward

You'll get a lot of pedal power in this position, but it places a lot of stress on the larger muscles and can cause fatigue and tightness in the upper leg.

About right

You should be able to pass a vertical line (use a bit of string and a weight for a plumb line) through the center of your knee (the bony lump just behind your knee cap) and the pedal spindle when the cranks are parallel to the ground.

Trail shock

The ups and downs of the trail are always going to place excessive strain on your body – in short, you have to put up with the battering that your bike does, but your bike's built to take it and you're not. Suspension can work wonders for some people's problems as it can often reduce the bashes, but it does also mean extra work (in the case of full suspension) on the climbs. This can lead to fatigue-induced back pain. Suspension shock posts are a good idea if you can't afford a new bike and if your back ache is worse after a really rough ride. Always remember to use your arms and knees to help absorb the big hits on the descents and try to remain relaxed and comfortable on the climbs.

Setting your bike up for the trail

Preride safety checks

The best preride safety measure is to wash your bike after every ride (see pages 43–45). Washing your bike means you get up close to it, so you'll notice damage like cracks and dents and will also be able to inspect the derailleurs, chains and brakes for wear and tear. Always spin the wheels and check the wobbles by watching them pass the brake pads; any wear on the rims should be checked too. Also check out anything unusual, like noises and creaks.

Following are 10 safety checks that you should always carry out before setting off on a ride.

1. The frame
Regular crashes add to fatigue and can lead to the frame going out of alignment or becoming bent. Look out for cracks around the welds, ripples or folds around the head tube and flaking paint, as they are all signs that the tube underneath has been twisted out of shape. If your bike has a steel frame, be aware of rust spots as these can be a sign of further damage on the inside of the frame tubes. See pages 145–48 for more on frame alignment.

2a. Suspension systems
First, make sure you are aware of what type of fork you have (see pages 135–36). To check the fork action, apply the front brake and give the forks a few pumps – you are looking out for 'stiction' or a notchy feedback to the movement. Also note the rebound speed – if it is very slow there may be a loss in pressure or a spring failure. You can adjust the rebound and compression speed on most varieties of fork. See pages 136–39 for more on fork setup and maintenance.

2b. Rear shocks and suspension
Make regular inspections of the bearings and pivots. Keep the air pressure in the shock consistent to maintain the ride quality and place less strain on the moving parts. A depressurized shock out on the trail can damage the frame if you have to ride home, so consider taking a shock pump on the ride for emergencies, especially if you are going to be miles from home. See pages 140–42 for more on rear shock maintenance.

3. Tire pressure

Tire pressure is always printed on the sidewall of the tire. All types of inner tubes and valves leak air gradually; some of the lightweight latex tubes and UST tubeless tires can lose as much as 20 per cent of their pressure overnight, so always check your tire pressure. Use a workshop floor pump with an accurate pressure gauge if you can. Also inspect the treads for thorns, flints and glass, which may have become lodged in the tread. See pages 101–6 for more on tires and tubes.

4. Brakes and headset

Check for disc (or rim) and pad wear. This is especially important in wet weather. On V-brakes the pads also wear out the rims, which now have wear indicators. It's important to keep an eye out for this, as if your rims wear through they can split, which usually results in a nasty tire blow-out.

   The brake pads have a line on them to denote permissible wear. Disc brakes are less susceptible to wear in the wet, but keep an eye on them as a lack of power and a slack feeling at the lever can mean the pads need replacing. At the same time, check the headset is tight by holding on to the front brake and rocking the bike slightly forward and backward. This will tell you if the headset is loose. See pages 69–88 for more on brakes and pages 123–29 for more on headsets.

5. Handlebars

Make sure that the handlebars are tight and check for bends or scratches. The basic rule is: if it's bent or scratched, trash it. Bends and scratches are both signs of fatigue – a bend will eventually snap and a scratch will act as a stress riser, which, given time and enough abuse, will eventually fail. Also check the bars, handlebar stem, steerer pinch bolts and bar-end bolts for tightness. See pages 91–93 for more on bar and stem setup.

6. Contact points

Contact points are where you rest your hands, feet and backside on the bike, and are the load-bearing components:
   · saddle fixing bolts on seatpost
   · seatpost binder bolt
   · pedals and crank bolts
   · handlebars and controls.
These components can loosen so check them before each ride and tighten if necessary. Do not overtighten, as over-stressed nuts and bolts are more likely to fail under impact. Use a torque wrench to check they are tightened to the manufacturers' recommended torque figures. See pages 91–99 for more on contact points.

7. Pedals

Clean out your cleats if you use SPD clipless-type pedals, and keep the mechanism on the pedal clean and well lubricated. If it's muddy, spray some Teflon lube onto them to help shed mud and keep them sweet in the wet. See pages 95–99 for more on pedal care.

8. Chain and cassette

Check the chain and cassette for wear and always apply fresh lube before you ride: wet oil for muddy and wet conditions and a dry Teflon lube for dusty summer trails. Clean the chain regularly too, as it will last far longer and shift better if it's not covered in dirt. Always run through the gears to check that they index properly and make sure all the cables move freely and aren't bent. See pages 53–64 for more on gear setup and pages 65–67 for more on chain and cassette care.

9. Front and rear wheel quick-release mechanisms

Check that the front and rear wheel quick-release mechanisms are tight. If you arrive at the trail head in a car, chances are you will have to put the wheels back on the bike before you start riding. It's worth double-checking that they are tight, especially if you use disc brakes. Also, if you are racing it's worth checking you have done them up, as wheels often drop out on the start line. See pages 32–34 for more on removing wheels.

10. Tool kit and spares

Lastly, don't forget to take your trail tools and spares with you. See pages 13–14 for more on recommended trail tools.

On-the-trail fixes

When the first mountain bikers hit the dirt over 20 years ago, there were loads of strange suggestions for repairs on the trail using pieces of wood, old tin cans and bits of bail twine. In those days the bikes had to be fixed somehow, as the components were not really built for off-road abuse, but these repairs are really only for entertainment value now – they are pretty ineffectual and shouldn't be attempted. In fact, the modern mountain bike is very tough, with each part designed to survive extreme weather and riding abuse.

So, don't worry too much – breakdowns are unlikely to happen unannounced, as long as you conduct regular preride checks (see pages 25–27) and clean your bike frequently. The key to trouble-free riding is being able to spot accidents before they happen.

Riding alone

Riding alone is inevitable. If you intend to ride all day, it's always better to ride with a group, but if it can't be avoided remember to tell someone where you are going and how long you'll be. You must remember to cover any breakdown eventuality and carry sufficient tools and spares to get you home. Take a cell phone with you too, although you don't have to turn it on all the time if you want a peaceful ride. Do keep in mind, however, that when riding in remote areas cell phone service may be scant to none.

Top 10 on-the-trail tips

1. On very long rides, take some lube with you. Use it on your chain and derailleurs, especially if it's muddy or really dusty.
2. If you flat, *take your time*. Make sure you check several times for thorns in the tire before you fix the tube or replace it.
3. Always repair and reuse tubes.
4. Repair tubes on the trail if you have time, as you might need the spare for a more serious tube disaster later on.
5. Don't put a twig in your stem to use as a replacement handlebar – walk home or catch the bus if your bike is unrideable.
6. Stuffing your tires with twigs and trail debris is an okay idea if home isn't too far away and you're on smooth terrain. And you have a sense of humor.
7. Take your trash and bits of broken bike home with you.
8. Remember to secure your tool kit so you don't scatter your favorite tools all over your favorite trail.
9. If you go on big adventure rides, take all the tools you would need to strip everything, and carry First Aid supplies.
10. Close gates, smile at hikers and don't race deer – they're fast and unpredictable...

Top 10 trail fails

1. Punctures

Cause: A fact of life if you ride off-road. Thorns, sharp stones, nails, barbed wire, glass and so on can all cause punctures.
Prevention: Run tires at their recommended pressures (see sidewall of tire). Check tire treads for glass and similar intrusions that could work through the tire and cause a flat. Replace tires regularly.
Trail fix: Always carry two spare tubes and a puncture kit. If you are really stuck, tie a tight knot in the tube on either side of the hole, which might get you home. See pages 35–40 for more on how to fix a flat.

2. Tire disasters

Cause: Gashes from rocks and trail debris, or the brake block rubbing on the sidewall for a long time.
Prevention: Check tires for wear and replace regularly. Run tires at their recommended pressures.
Trail fix: Tire boots are available, which can patch the inside of the tire if it has a rip in it. You can also use big puncture patches and stiff cardboard (milk carton cardboard is good for this). See pages 35–40 for more on how to fix a flat.

3. Broken chain

Cause: Twisting strain on links of the chain, usually when straining a gear shift and pedaling with great force, or a poorly installed or poor-quality chain.
Prevention: Use a quality chain and replace it regularly. Use a chain checker to ensure it isn't stretched. Use gears that keep as straight a chainline as possible – middle chainring and middle of the cassette is best.
Trail fix: Always carry a spare link for a SRAM-brand chain (and/or a spare pin if you use Shimano chains) and a good-quality chain tool. See pages 65–67 for more on how to replace a chain.

4. Broken spokes

Cause: Usually uneven tension in the spokes, which normally happens when the wheel is reaching the end of its life.
Prevention: Regular checkups with a competent wheelbuilder, and having good wheels built in the first place with regular tension.
Trail fix: Folding 'cable spokes' are available, which can fold away into a tool kit. See pages 107–11 for more on how to true a wheel and replace a spoke.

5. Rim/wheel failure

Cause: Crashes, poor build, loose spokes and big hits. Rims can wear through and the bead can detach from the rim, which can be catastrophic!
Prevention: Look for wear and dents in the rim and check spoke tension. Regular brake pad and rim checkups will also help prevent on-the-trail failures.
Trail fix: This depends on the severity of the problem, and might mean a long walk home. Wheels *can* be re-straightened with brute force, but only if a spoke wrench can't do the job. See pages 109–11 for more on wheel maintenance.

6. Gear cable failure

Cause: Forcing the gear to shift, or simple wear and tear.
Prevention: Keep the cables lubricated and free-running. Replace cables (inners and outers) regularly.
Trail fix: The gear stops can be adjusted to run in a suitable single gear to get you home, or you can clamp the cable under a bottle boss bolt. Or carry a spare. See pages 57–64 for more on how to adjust derailleurs and replace gear cables.

7. Brake cable failure

Cause: This is rare, but brake cables can fray and break.
Prevention: Use quality cables and replace them regularly.
Trail fix: Carry spare cables, one for the brakes and one for the gears. See pages 73–75 for more on how to replace brake cables.

8. Freewheel failure

Cause: Broken pawls in the freehub/cassette body.
Prevention: Regular servicing and replacement, if necessary.
Trail fix: Secure the cassette to the spokes with zip ties and you can ride home with a crudely fixed gear. See pages 115–17 for more on how to replace cassette bodies.

9. Rear derailleur failure

Cause: The derailleur can get stuck in the spokes and break, or get damaged after a crash.
Prevention: Always check that the rear derailleur is straight and can't touch the spokes when you're in the lowest gear.
Trail fix: Remove the rear derailleur and go 'singlespeed'. See pages 53–67 for more on how to service gears and chains.

10. Chain suck

Cause: Either worn chainrings or chain. The chain can get trapped onto the chainring and jammed into the frame.
Prevention: Replace the chain regularly and fit a new chainring as soon as possible.
Trail fix: Try to use the big chainring to get home. See pages 53–67 for more on how to service gears and chains.

Other potential problems

The following are less likely to happen, but it's worth knowing the trailside solutions just in case.

The cranks snap or loosen off

This is a pretty rare occurrence and is usually due to neglect or a poor-quality set of cranks. Usually, cracks appear first, so keep a close eye on them. Carry the correct size Allen key or wrench to fit the bolts, as loose cranks ruin themselves very quickly if you ride on them for even a short space of time. If your cranks keep running loose, this means that the taper cut-out in the crank has worn out and it is time to replace it.

The pedals get smashed or fall off

It is possible to ride with one foot, but it is a bit uncomfortable. I've heard of riders riding for miles with a twig stuffed in the crank threads to support their foot. You could try this in an emergency – but only in an emergency.

The stem snaps or bends

This is pretty rare these days, but when it does happen it is usually terminal. Don't attempt to ride a bent or cracked stem, and if you notice it failing during a ride then catch the bus home. Munching the broken end of a stem is highly uncomfortable.

The bars snap or bend

If you really need to, you can get home using just one side of the bar if you shift it through the stem and just use one brake lever or stuff a broom handle in there, but this is asking for trouble if you've got to ride any distance. If you try to ride downhill with the bar in this state, you'll be in a hospital quicker than you can say 'look Mom – no hands!' Bent bars are just waiting to snap, so if you have a bad crash and they get bent replace them – especially if they are lightweight.

Seatpost and/or bolt failure

This is fairly common. It usually means that the bolt has rusted through or has been overtightened. The obvious cure is to keep an eye on the neglected area and make sure you grease all the threads. Also, check the post after crashes or bad landings for slight bends – hold a ruler alongside it and, if it's even slightly bent, change it.

The headset loosens

Threadless headsets usually just need a simple Allen key tweak, but old-style headsets can be tightened with a toestrap or a reusable zip tie.

The frame snaps

This usually means that you're walking home. Don't try to get creative with coat hangers or foliage, just plan your letter to the warranty department and call a friend. Riding broken frames will be very dangerous, possibly fatal, so don't try it. Bent frames are just waiting to snap, so if your frame looks like it's bent get it checked out by a mechanic or frame builder.

Pretzeled wheel

If the buckle is incurable with a spoke wrench, try standing on it and get one of your riding buddies to stand on the other side of the buckle. Then you can jump up and down on the other side – even if it doesn't work it'll keep you warm while someone goes for help. This is a last resort – the wheel may pop back into shape, but this will probably ruin the rim and the spokes. Obviously, most slight buckles can be fixed with a spoke wrench and a bit of practice. I suggest picking up the rudiments of wheel truing before riding extreme terrain or long trail rides.

The derailleurs(s) snap or get mashed up

Rear derailleurs can fail at the cage or the springs can give up. Sometimes the derailleur gets smashed off in a bad crash, which can also bend the rear hanger. A lot of frames have replaceable rear hangers, but if yours doesn't then fit a breakaway bolt that will snap off before your dropout. If either derailleur fails, it's best to remove it completely. If it's the front derailleur, put the chain on the middle ring and if it's the rear derailleur, shorten the chain to fit a medium-sized sprocket on the cassette, then ride home single speed – it's great fun!

A valve snaps

This can happen if you try to pump your tires up in a hurry and is another good reason to carry (at least) two spare tubes.

Fork failure

Fork failure is a very scary subject. Suspension forks are usually built to handle punishment but they can fail internally, which usually means a slow ride home. If rigid forks fail, it can mean a ride home in an ambulance. However, forks usually only break following a previous crash and if they are bent first.

Brake failure

This falls into two categories: pad failure and cable failure. You should spot pad failure before they wear out, and cable failures can be repaired if you remember to take a spare. If you haven't, don't try using bits of string as they will only get caught in the wheel. If you still use canti-brakes, get the rear one to work – if it's busted you should sacrifice the front brake to patch up the rear one.

Full suspension failures

These depend very much on how severe the failure is. As with all bikes, if the frame fails then it's very dangerous to ride it. If the shock fails you can usually ride home without too many problems, but you risk damaging the suspension unit or the frame so take it easy.

The chainring bends

The chainring can usually be bent back with some gentle persuasion (a big rock) or with a pair of pliers. A chainring tooth will break off quite easily, however, so don't force it.

Removing wheels

The standard mountain bike wheel has a quick-release mechanism (QR). This system is excellent for removing the wheels instantly, which is great for repairing punctures or putting your bike in the back of your car. But to the uninitiated they can be potentially hazardous if done incorrectly. On most mountain bikes the front-wheel system has a slightly different technique from the rear-wheel system. If you are removing both wheels, take the front one out first; this will make the bike easier to manage and means that you won't have to drag the chain and gears on the ground.

Before you start, if your bike has V-brakes, unhook the brakes (see page 22 for help). This is to ensure the tire clears the brake pads and falls out cleanly. You don't need to do this if your bike has disc brakes, as the wheels will simply drop out.

Quick-release lever

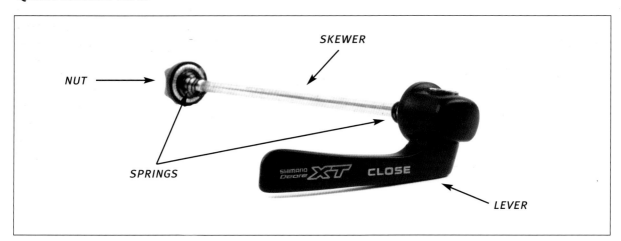

NUT

SKEWER

SPRINGS

SHIMANO Deore XT   CLOSE

LEVER

Important note

Tightening the QR adequately is essential for safety if you have disc brakes, especially on the front wheel. This is mainly because they are more effective than rim brakes and as such place more stress on the wheel and therefore the hub. This twisting in the wheel can loosen the quick release, but only if it is installed incorrectly. Obviously, this needs to be checked regularly, especially before and after rides.

Also, be careful where you position the lever in the closed position. If it faces forwards or down, it can catch on undergrowth and come undone. Place the front QR so that it runs behind the fork, and the rear one in line with the seat stay (pointing towards the saddle). This will also make it easier to undo the lever.

Front wheels

1 'Lawyer tabs' are designed to prevent the wheel from falling out should the quick-release (QR) lever be done up too loosely. They are called 'lawyer tabs' because of several well-publicized U.S. lawsuits in the early days of the mountain bike. A few companies were sued over front wheels dropping out of the forks unannounced, which had catastrophic results. But, to be fair, this was more to do with poor installation than mechanical failure. This is why there is a big disclaimer sticker on the bike telling you to do up your QRs before your first ride.

2 Once the QR is undone the wheel will still not drop out, so the nut on the non-lever side needs to be loosened a little more. The key here is to remember how much you have undone it and not to remove it completely. To clear the tabs, undo the nut; three full turns will be enough on most bikes. The wheel will then drop out.

3 The springs on the inside of the quick-release mechanism help centralize the nut and the lever to push them away from the bike. They also make it easier to replace the wheel, as you don't have to center the assembly. This leaves your hands free to hold the bike and the wheel.

4 The front wheel has to be firmly placed into the dropouts before you can do up the lever. For this reason I suggest you replace the wheels with the bike on the ground; this way the weight of the bike can help make the wheels go in straight.

Rear wheels

1 The chain should be on the smallest sprocket (or cog) and the largest chainring, so make sure you change into this gear before you start. This makes it easier to get the chain off the cassette and easier to replace the wheel afterward.

2 Stand behind the bike and hold the bike upright with your legs trapping the wheel, leaving your hands free to remove the wheel. Now undo the lever.

3 The wheel will remain trapped into the bike by the chain, so twist the derailleur backward to release the wheel. The chain should stay on the front chainwheel, so it will be easier if you start with the chain in this position when you replace the wheel.

4 To replace the rear wheel, the derailleur needs to spring into the correct position with the wheel in the bike. Next, wrap the chain over the top of the smallest sprocket to help the wheel slot into the dropouts. Take care to line the disc brake up centrally to the pads in the caliper.

5 Pull the wheel upward and backward, and it should slot into place easily. If it doesn't, the wheel may have become snagged on the brake pads or the derailleur may not be in the correct gear position.

6 Do not adjust the nut on the QR lever as the rear wheel should clear the dropouts and slip in easily. However, it is worth checking that the lever feels tight as it closes. Rest your weight on the bike as this will keep the wheel central in the rear dropouts.

Doing up the quick-release lever (both wheels)

Once the wheel is slotted into the dropouts (or fork ends), slowly tighten the nut up until the lever starts to tighten. When the lever is directly in line with the skewer, as shown here, that is enough – this will ensure that the lever will close tightly enough.

Fixing a flat

Punctures are a fact of mountain bike life, no matter how hard you try to avoid them. Prevention can only be aided by running your tires at their recommended pressures and replacing them regularly. Also, always use the right tire for the terrain you are going to ride on. Fatter tires don't prevent pierce-type punctures, but they can be run at slightly lower pressures than thinner tires to avoid a pinch flat. Narrower tires can cut through mud, but need to be pumped up harder, which means you lose grip and comfort.

Replacing a tire can be done quickly after practice, but it's worth taking your time if you can as you will be less likely to make a mistake and risk flatting another tube. Also, try to get the tire reinflated as close as you can to the recommended pressure; even if your mini-pump takes forever, it will help prevent another flat.

Tubeless tires are less likely to puncture, but they can still suffer serious gashes and do occasionally flat. They can be repaired with a tire boot or a patch kit. Most flats on UST tires can be repaired with a standard tube. See pages 103–6 for more on tubeless tires.

Tools required:
· **tire levers**
· **spare tube (or puncture kit)**
· **mini-pump**

On the trail

1 As soon as you realize you have a flat, stop. It's better to get on with fixing the flat than trying to ride any farther on a potentially hazardous wheel. Riding with a flat can also damage the rim should you hit anything hard on the trail. Stopping straight away may also allow you to find the hole in the tire and remove any sharp objects that may have become trapped in the tread. Remove the wheel and hang your bike up on a suitable bush or tree branch. If the puncture is in the rear wheel, try not to dangle the chain in the mud. See pages 32–34 for more on removing wheels.

2 Most mountain bike tires are quite loose fitting. Although the photograph shows two tire levers being used to remove the tire, most off-road mountain bike tires will come off easily with just one. Push the tire away to reveal the bead (the part of the tire around the edge that recesses into the rim), slip the lever tip under the bead and simply pull the bead off. If you have to use two levers, pull one section off first and then move a little further around the rim. The second lever will be harder to pull, but should pop the tire off easily. Run the lever around the rim, which will remove one side of the tire from the rim. **Do not remove the tire completely at this point.**

3 Pull the tube away from the tire and pack it away – you can fix it later. Check that there is nothing wrong with the rim tape beneath the tube, as it can sometimes come loose under the tire and move, exposing a spoke hole that can pinch the tube.

4 Double-check the tire walls for thorns and anything that may have penetrated the tire. Be careful not to get any trail debris in there either, as it may be sharp and cause another flat on inflation. If there is a large gash in the sidewall you may have to use a tire patch; you can improvise one using a piece of cardboard, but the best option is a patch that can be stuck to the inside of the tire. This is just a temporary fix until you can get a new tire.

5 Slightly inflate the replacement tube with two strokes of a mini-pump, just enough for the tube to take shape but not so much that it becomes bigger than the diameter of the wheel. Next, insert the valve into the valve hole. Make sure that the valve is seated properly into the rim, then push the tire over the top of the tube.

6 Work the tube carefully into the carcass of the tire – if you are having difficulties, try inflating it slightly. Beware of folds in the tube at this point and do not twist the tube as you return it to the tire, as this can pinch and even puncture once the tire is reinflated; it also means that the tire will inflate unevenly.

7 You should tuck the tube so it sits inside the tire carcass but, more importantly, away from the rim. Leaving any part of the tube outside the tire makes it very difficult to replace the tire without pinching the tube.

8 Now, start to return the tire bead into the rim. Start opposite the valve hole and work the tire either side with two hands, until there is only a small amount left. The last part of the tire can be pulled onto the rim by hand, which can be a bit of a struggle depending on the rim and tire model. However, it is best to pull it on this way as using a tire lever can pinch the tube as you lever it on. If you can't manage it ask someone to help – four hands are better than two!

9 Once the tire is back on the rim, check that the bead hasn't snagged the tube, or that part of the tube isn't trapped between the bead and the rim. This can push the tire off the rim or make it roll unevenly, or even explode once the tire has been pumped up to a decent pressure if the bead is pinched under the rim. This really makes you jump!

10 Finally, pump the tire up to the recommended pressure. If the tire doesn't run true (it wobbles as you spin the wheel), reseat it by letting most of the air out and pulling the tire away from the bead. This will help the bead sit into the rim and usually 'pops' the tire into place. See pages 38–39 for more on mini-pumps.

TOP TIRE TIPS

- Swap the front tire with the back tire on a regular basis. This will help your tires last longer as the rear tire wears faster than the front.
- Some pro-racers carry a partially inflated tube in their rear pocket, so replacing a tube takes less time.
- Many racers practice fixing a flat, as punctures can mean losing important time and therefore races. World Cup riders can fix a flat in well under a minute, which is pretty good going – how quickly can you fix one?!
- Selecting the right tire is like selecting the right golf club – semi-slicks are going to be useless in the mud and cross-country tires won't last long on a jump bike. As a rule, use fat tires with plenty of tread. They last longer, puncture less and are far more comfortable than skinny ones.
- New tires can have a residue on them that can make them a bit slippery. A muddy ride and a proper wash with degreaser will remove this pretty quickly.

Tire know-how

- **Knobs** – square or shaped tread elements.
- **Directional tread** – a tread shaped to assist drive (arrows on the sidewall show which way to place them).
- **PSI** – pounds per square inch (pressure measurement).
- **BAR** – international pressure measurement.
- **UST** – tubeless tire system first developed by Mavic.
- **26 x 1.5–2.5 inches** – the standard measurements for off-road tires.
- **Wire bead** – steel bead that retains the tire in the rim.
- **Kevlar bead** – lighter folding version of the wire bead, which is also easier to remove from the rim.
- **Kevlar belted tires** – puncture reinforcement to prevent pierce punctures.
- **Snakebite protection** – reinforced sidewalls to help prevent pinch punctures.

Patching a puncture and using a mini-pump

I have about 20-odd punctures every year, so mending them is far cheaper than using a new tube every time.

   Many riders carry at least two spare tubes all the time, and it's far better to replace the tube than try to patch it if you are out on the trail. Who wants to wait for the glue to dry off or try to keep the patches dry? Fixing tubes is best done in the dry as it can take around ten minutes to mend each hole. If you use a decent puncture kit it's highly unlikely that the patch will leak; in fact, Rema feathered-edge patches are actually stronger than the tube itself. However, if you are out on the trail it's far better to have several spare tubes with you so you can get back on your bike quickly and not hold anyone up.

Tools required:

- **mini-pump**
- **sandpaper**
- **glue**
- **patch**
- **talc (optional)**

1 Find the hole. This is usually a case of pumping up the tube and listening. A bucket of water is not required for this – just keep pumping until you can hear the 'psssssss'. Once you have the hole, place your finger and thumb over it as you don't want to lose it.

2 Rough up the area around the hole with some sandpaper. This will help the glue penetrate the rubber and ensure the patch adheres properly. The glue is a contact adhesive (it works when the patch is placed on it), but needs to be applied to a grease-free and dry tube in order to work properly.

3 Apply plenty of glue to the area, starting at the hole and working outwards. Keep an eye on where the hole is so you can get the patch over it properly later on. Leave the glue for 5 minutes until it is almost completely dry.

4 Most fixable holes can be covered by a 2-cm patch. Apply firm pressure to the patch with your thumb, as you want the patch to be fully in place before you reinflate. Stretch the tube gently by pulling either side of the patch – this will show if it has stuck. If it's a pinch flat (or snakebite puncture – see page 40) use two patches (one over each hole) rather than one big one.

5 Remove the plastic backing film from the center. Do not pull it off from a corner as it can pull the patch off with it. The backing is used to make sure you don't touch the underside of the patch and so you can press it onto the tube easily.

6 If you can dust the area with talc, this will prevent the glue from sticking to the inside of the tire and help it slide into place as you inflate the tire.

7 Undo the small locking tip of the valve (Presta type only). Free it up by pressing it in a couple of times; this will enable the valve to pass air in easily as sometimes it gets 'stuck' after full inflation.

8 Push the pump head firmly onto the valve. Sometimes you will have to place a thumb behind the tire to prevent the valve vanishing into the hole as you push it home (some valves have lock rings to prevent this).

9 All good mini-pumps have a locking lever. This ensures that the pump head makes an airtight seal over the valve and means you can concentrate on inflating the tire. The valve internals can be removed and replaced as they wear out. The seal can also be swapped around to cope with either valve type (see your pump instructions as this depends on the make).

10 Pump firmly but don't rush. If you push too hard or at an awkward angle you can bend the valve or snap the locking part off. Use all of the pumping stroke and take your time. Make sure you pump the tire up to the recommended pressure to prevent further punctures and allow you to ride just as hard.

Tire boot

Large tire gashes need to be repaired because the tube will blister out of any holes in the tire and explode again. You can use an empty energy gel packet or a piece of cardboard to cover the hole, but tire boots are better as they stick to the inside of the tire and don't slip as you reinflate it.

'Glueless' patches

Although not as permanent as the glue and patch variety, glueless patches can provide an emergency fix and work especially well if you are in a rush or if it's raining, as you don't have to wait for the glue to dry. As with standard patches, sand the area properly to help the patch fix to the tube.

Snakebite punctures

Snakebite punctures occur when you have smacked something pretty hard (usually a rock, curb or sharp tree root) and the tube is pinched between the object and the rim, making two holes on either rim edge – hence 'snakebite' as it looks like two teeth have punctured your tube. These are hard to fix as you will usually need two patches – one to cover each hole.

Valve types

Presta (thin-type) or Schraeder (car-type) valves both have their benefits. Presta valves can handle greater pressures and don't leak as much as Schraeder valves. However, Schraeder valves are easier to pump up and you can always top them up at a gas station. The core can be replaced in most Schraeder valves and some Presta valves if they are leaking.

Transporting your bike

You have several options for transporting your bike – in your car, on a trunk rack, on a roof rack or in a travel bag. Some are better than others...

In your car

The safest way to carry your bike is in the back of your car. First, remove both the wheels (see pages 32–34). If you have hydraulic disc brakes, place a spacer between the pads just in case you activate the levers when placing your bike in the boot. Wrap the chain and rear derailleur in a cloth so as not to get oil all over the place.

Try to pack your bike last and on top of all your other kit and lay the wheels under the frame. It's a good idea to get some wheel bags (trash bags are good too), especially if it's been muddy or wet. Try not to let the tires rub on anything sharp or you'll have a nasty shock when the sidewalls wear a hole and puncture.

On a roof rack

Remove all loose-fitting equipment, such as drink bottles, tool packs, pumps and so on. Fasten the front wheel into the wheel clamp. Give the fork leg a good shake to ensure it's tight. Fasten the rear wheel strap and you're set. Before you drive off, double-check that all the straps are tight and you haven't left anything on the floor around the car or on top of the roof.

If you stop for anything, lock the bikes to the rack (most racks now have lockable fork fastenings) and always use a roof rack with lockable roof brackets. Lastly, don't go into a height-limited parking garage as this will ruin your bike, car and roof rack. And yes, it does happen more often than you might think!

On a trunk rack

Trunk racks are not ideal. Many retro-fit to the car with straps and rest on bumpers and rear windows, and are therefore not suited to carrying heavy bikes or more than two. They scratch your car and can, in time, damage the rear windows. The best type of trunk rack is one that fits to the tow bar or, like the one pictured here, is a permanent fitting. If you have a heavy down-hill rig, it's far safer to put it inside the car.

In a travel bag

First, remove the pedals and the saddle and seatpost. Wrap these up in a plastic bag and place them straight into the bag or into your hand luggage – don't leave them on the kitchen table. It can ruin your vacation if the airline sends your bike somewhere else, so I usually pack my helmet, saddle, shoes and pedals in my hand luggage so at least I can rent a bike when I get there as I'll have all my familiar contact points with me.

1 Remove the wheels and take out the quick-release skewers. It's worth letting the tires down almost completely – they shouldn't explode in the hold but it's better to be safe. I leave a little air in just to protect the rims and to provide some more padding. Place the wheels in the bag and tape them to one another, or use electrical zip ties. Space them so that the cassette and axle will not damage the frame. Cover the ends of the axle with cardboard to prevent them causing any damage inside the bag.

2 Remove the handlebars (whether or not you have to do this will depend on the type of bag you are using). If you are packing your bike in a bike box, you may well have to remove the bars to fold the bike flat. If you do, tighten the bolts that you have removed to prevent losing them and wrap the bars in bubble wrap. Tape anything like this in place with duct tape as it will damage your paintwork and ruin components if it rattles around.

3 Remove the rear derailleur. This is worth doing as it's vulnerable and is one less thing to be sticking out and risk getting bent as your bike is thrown into the hold. Wrap it up in a plastic bag along with the chain. Duct tape it to the rear triangle, safely out of the way.

4 Use plenty of pipe lagging (insulating tubes) to protect the frame and forks. Wrap some around the suspension forks and the cranks too, as it absorbs a lot of shock. Lastly, don't forget to pack your pump, tools and, most important, a pedal wrench.

4 REGULAR CLEANING

Washing and caring for your bike

To keep your bike running smoothly and ensure that the components will last, wash your bike at least once a week – especially in the winter. Washing your bike is a great way to get close to it and inspect every aspect of its workings. Water gets into everything and therefore into all the sensitive parts of your bike, so it's best to wash your bike with care. Wear some rubber boots, rubber gloves and waterproof clothing, as you will then be able to concentrate on the job properly.

Pressure (jet) washers are certainly quick, but are also lazy and generally not a good idea for cleaning your bike as they tend to blow water into sealed units such as the headsets, forks, hubs and bottom brackets. They also ruin your cables and blow all the lubricant off your chain. Worse still, with com-

AND MAINTENANCE

plicated full suspension linkages, which can easily be neglected, the water will quickly turn bearings to rust and seize up your pivots and bushings. So, it's far better to hand-wash your bike with a sponge and brush; this way your bike will last longer and perform better.

Find a suitable area to clean your bike. Be aware that you will need plenty of water and that the by-products from a mountain bike can be quite messy. Therefore, a concrete area with a water supply and a drain is best. Always clean the floor with a stiff brush when you have finished as the degreasing fluids can make the floor very slippery.

Cleaning tools:
- water
- bucket
- brushes (large to toothbrush size)
- portable workstand
- spray-on bike wash
- strong degreaser (citrus ones are good) for drivetrain parts
- sponge
- chain-cleaning device
- sprocket cleaner (narrow brush to get between gaps)

1 Always clean the underside of the saddle and the seatpost first. This is so you can place the bike into the work stand before you wash the rest of your bike (most work stand clamps hold the seatpost) and also because it's best to start at the top of the bike and work down, so you don't get muck on stuff you have already washed.

2 Use a brush and a sponge to get the worst of the mud off. If you are using a hose, it's best to do this while the bike is still wet – once the mud is dry it gets far harder to shift. If you have space in your car, take your cleaning kit and a jug of water with you when you travel to the trails or races, so you can wash your bike before the dirt has a chance to do any damage.

3 Remove both of the wheels as they are far easier to clean when they are out of the bike. This will also give you access to the inside of the rear triangle and swing arm mechanism, and will allow you to swing the bike around easily in the workstand.

4 Place a chain guide in the drop-out and wrap the chain over it. This will help you clean the bike and chain, let you rotate the chain and cranks easily and keep the chain out of the way as you wash the rest of the bike. See pages 65–67 for more on chain care.

5 Place your bike in a stand at a suitable height, so you can wash the bike without bending down too much. Soak the loose mud off first, then cover your bike in bike-washing fluid. Leave this to soak in for a few moments.

6 Use a spray-on degreaser. You can dilute these cleaning sprays as they tend to be quite concentrated and powerful, and can even go 50:50 with many of them. Be careful to read the instructions as these fluids can be caustic and affect the finish of your bike. Most are not too kind to your hands either, so it's best to wear rubber gloves.

7 Wash the tires and use a stiff brush to knock the mud out of the tread. If you have V-brakes, pay particular attention to the rims, clean off all the black brake crud and inspect the rims for wear. Use an alcohol-based disc brake cleaning fluid on the rotors and be careful not to spread grease from any brushes you may have used on the cassette. This will contaminate the rotor or the pads and give you plenty of braking problems the next time you ride.

8 Be careful when cleaning the forks – don't spray degreaser directly at the seals and clean them with a sponge rather than a stiff brush. Spraying water and degreaser into the fork internals will cause problems in the future.

9 Rear suspension systems can collect a lot of mud. If you don't clean the mud off, it can corrode and seize the pivots. Inspect the shock for leaks and signs of wear and tear.

10 Also take special care when cleaning disc brakes as they can become contaminated with dirty oil and lubricant residue from the drivetrain. Use a clean brush and water to clean off the discs. With V-brakes you need to remove all the crud from the pads and inspect them for grit, which may have got stuck in the slots in the pad and need to be pried out. Inspect the rims for grooves where there may be wear from the pads.

11 Clean out the pedals and the shoe cleats using a smaller, toothbrush-size brush. Pay special attention to the cleats if you have been walking a lot on your muddy rides, as impacted mud will make the cleats malfunction. Knock the mud out or pry it out with a screwdriver as the cleats need to be clean to work properly. Keep the pedal springs well lubricated and check their tension regularly.

12 Clean all the muck out of the sprockets with a suitable implement. There are such things as sprocket cleaners, but you can just use a stiff brush. It is very important to keep the cassette clean so sometimes it's worth removing it and giving it a thorough clean. You can then clean and inspect the hubs too.

PRO TIPS

- If you are riding in really muddy conditions, spray the frame and drivetrain with extra spray lube such as GT85 or Shimano Chain Spray. This will prevent the mud from sticking so much and means you can ride for a little longer before having to stop. Be careful not to contaminate the disc pads when doing this.
- Use 1-inch strips of fabric to clean between the sprockets. T-shirt neck hems (the folded over bits) are particularly good for this job.
- If you have to use a jet wash, use it for the tires, saddle and frame only. Wash the rest of the bike by hand.
- Use a bike-wash detergent on all but the really stubborn muck. You can use car shampoo or washing-up liquid, but be careful as this can be corrosive and damage the paint. The concentrated and stronger degreasers (usually the citrus type) are best saved for the chains, chainrings and cassettes.

Cleaning and lubricating

The key to proper lubrication is to clean the component before you add any oil. Oiling an already mucky bike will just attract more muck, and cleaning components regularly will keep them running for a long time.

The modern bicycle's chain and gear system is finely tuned. Because the gearbox of a bike is external and therefore open to the elements, it gets a fair amount of abuse. This assists in degrading and corroding all the moving metal parts. Basically, if you leave your bike out in the rain it will rust in a matter of hours, and if you leave the chain, suspension forks and rear shock covered in mud your bike will wear out pretty quickly. Lubrication helps prevent corrosion, but leaving a chain dirty and simply relubing it will just help attract more dirt. In the long term, this leads to a buildup of grunge and accelerated chain and sprocket wear.

So, clean your bike and degrease the chain completely on a regular (bi-weekly) basis. Use a water-repellent spray (GT85 is good) on the rust-sensitive parts and dry them off with a rag. Only use a bicycle-specific lubricant as some water-repellent sprays and lubricants have solvents in them that can damage the sensitive parts of your bike and ruin your paintwork. See pages 43–45 for more on bike cleaning.

Lubrication

Derailleur pulleys
Spraying lube all over the derailleur pulleys just attracts more crud to the chain and rear derailleur. If you have been riding a lot in wet weather, it's worth stripping the derailleur and regreasing the bushes inside the derailleur pulleys. See page 55 for more on replacing derailleur pulleys.

Canti studs
Spray a small amount of light dry oil behind the canti (V-brake) and onto the pivot. Obviously, do not spray the rims at the same time! Remove and regrease the studs on a regular basis as they are steel and will rust if exposed to lots of wet weather. See pages 69–88 for more on brake servicing.

Cables

Inner cables can be stripped out of the slotted cable guides and lubricated with a Teflon-based lubricant. You can use a heavier lubricant, but these can clog up after a while so use sparingly. If you ride in all weather conditions, or mainly in wet weather, fit a set of cable oilers, which allow you to blast the dirt and water out of the cables and keep them running free. They are very simple to fit and can be installed when you replace the cables. See pages 54–58 for more on cable replacement and servicing.

Chain

Clean the chain and use a dry lube in the summer and a wet lube in the winter or in wet weather. Use a water-repellent spray after washing and lube before every ride. See pages 65–67 for more on chain servicing.

Rear derailleur

Use a thin lube on the rear derailleur and drop some oil onto the pivots. Work this in by running through the gears a few times. Check the spring inside the derailleur as it should be clean and rust-free. See pages 53–64 for more on gear servicing.

Front derailleur

Like the rear derailleur, the front derailleur doesn't need soaking in buckets of heavy lube, but the pivots will benefit from a drop of dry lube squirted and worked into the moving parts. Wipe off any excess with a rag. See pages 59–61 for more on front derailleur setup.

Pedals

Clipless pedal mechanisms must be cleaned and lubricated regularly. They will clog up quickly if they are permanently dirty, so clean them if you have been riding (and walking) in mud. Clean the cleats in the shoes too as mud can get impacted into the soles and will prevent the cleats from releasing smoothly. See pages 95–97 for more on pedal servicing.

Brake levers

Like door hinges, brake levers benefit from a squirt of lube every now and again. Make sure that the cable nipple can move freely in the cable-retaining hole. If this goes dry, the friction can damage the lever or break the cable. See pages 69–88 for more on brake servicing.

Gear levers and Gripshift

It's best not to spray lots of sticky grunge into these sensitive (mainly plastic and nylon) components. A little light oil (dry lube) will keep the water out. Oil the gear levers and Gripshift sparingly and only occasionally. See pages 62–64 for more on Gripshift servicing.

Suspension forks

Never lubed your forks? Well, you should – a couple of drops of wet lube worked in with a couple of pumps on the bars will keep the seals sweet. See pages 130–42 for more on routine suspension servicing.

Suspension bikes

As with the forks, the rear suspension unit needs a drop of oil occasionally. The pivots and bushes also need a squirt of lube, especially after wet rides. See pages 130–42 for more on routine suspension servicing.

Cleaning the chain

1 Chain baths are the best option for cleaning a chain quickly and easily. Take the wheels out of the bike and place the chain on a chain retainer.

2 Clean in between the cassette sprockets and get all of the muck out of the derailleur pulleys on the derailleur. If you don't, the clean chain will get dirty again as soon as you replace the wheels and turn the pedals.

3 Fill the chain bath with a strong mixture of citrus degreaser and water.

4 Just hold onto the chain bath and rotate the pedals a few times to get a spotless chain – it's magic!

Squeaks and creaks

A persistent noise from your bike can drive you mad. Squeaks, ticks and creaks can originate from many different places and they often need a careful process of elimination to find the source of the noise. Noises mean that there is something wrong so take them seriously.

To understand and solve these noises you will need to read through the book, as a properly adjusted bike will be a silent one. However, the main cause of noise from your bike will be dry bearing surfaces or loose components. The friction between surfaces, whether at the threads in your bottom bracket or the clamp on your handlebars, will not be solved by spraying copious amounts of penetrating lubricant into the component – and in particular, don't do this to your handlebars as they could slip and cause a nasty accident. You can't always solve the problem simply by doing the bolts up a little tighter either, as they have recommended tightening torques and may simply need some anti-seize compound applying to them if they are titanium or aluminum. A persistent rubbing can be something as simple as a cable end hitting the cranks as you pedal, or something less obvious like a broken chain roller, a worn freewheel or a loose hub. All the components should be checked for cracks or splits, and anything that looks unusual should be checked out and replaced if necessary.

So what causes the noises in each component?

Saddle
Very often, the saddle is the cause of pedaling-related noises. As the saddle is usually exposed to the muck off the rear wheel, it gets a lot of abuse and very little cleaning or care. The rails can start to wear out, resulting in a nasty noise as you push on the pedals and move your weight across the saddle. This can be relieved with a spray lube, but the saddle may need replacing. The rails

---

How to detect where the noise is coming from

1. Stand on either pedal (you will need to be off the bike to do this) and apply some sideways pressure on the bottom bracket. If it clicks, the cranks or the bottom bracket may be the root of the noise.
2. Hold the front wheel in your knees and shake the bars from side to side – are the bars tight?
3. Apply the front brake and shake the bike – could the headset be loose?
4. Grab the saddle with both hands and twist it a little – is it the saddle or the seat post?
5. Shake the wheels – are the hubs loose?
6. When did you last service the gears or replace the chain?

---

can sometimes get corroded to the seatpost clamp, so check this out too.

Seatpost
A dry seatpost will seize up pretty quickly. The residue and corrosion inside the seat tube can make a nasty creaking sound. Remove the seatpost and carefully clean inside the seat tube. Seriously corroded seat tubes will need reaming (cleaning out with a specialist cutting tool). Clean the seatpost with some steel wool and reapply anti-seize grease before you replace it.

Seatpost clamp
The clamp needs to be a perfect fit and suitably tight. Quick-release seatpost clamps can cause problems if they are not secured tightly enough. If you don't adjust your saddle height as you ride, you could change the quick-release clamp for an Allen key fitting.

Bottom bracket

This is the biggest cause of noise and to solve any problems you will have to strip it out and rebuild it (see pages 152–53 for how to do this) on a regular basis.

Cranks

The usual cause of noise is the square taper-type bottom bracket, which can cause all sorts of problems if assembled incorrectly. Do not grease the taper as it simply forces the cranks on further and damages them. Clean the cranks with disc brake cleaner or a stronger degreaser and reassemble. Octalink-type bottom brackets need to be cleaned and a small amount of grease used to rebuild them. Always tighten to the correct torque setting and check for tightness regularly. See pages 155–57 for more on removing and replacing cranks.

Chainring bolts

These can often 'dry out' and start to click as a result. Remove them and clean the cranks thoroughly. Then rebuild the chainring bolts using an anti-seize compound.

Chainrings

Worn chainrings cause many more problems than you might think, and very often replacing the chain just makes them worse. Check the teeth for hook-shaped edges and missing teeth. A jumping chain can be dangerous – you'll get thrown forward as you pedal on the down stroke – so keep your chainrings in check.

Chain

This is often the cause of drivetrain noises. Check that the rollers of the chain are all intact and that there is no 'stiff link', which may also cause the chain to jump or skip across the sprockets.

Cassette body

Another cause of drivetrain noises: If the cassette body is old and worn out it will sound terrible. To check this, hold the largest sprocket and rock it from side to side; if there

is noticeable play then it may need replacing or tightening. Water and grit can ingress into the freewheel mechanism, which will eventually rust the internals.

Rear derailleur

Squeaks are usually associated with dry derailleur pulley bushings. If the squeak stops when you stop pedaling, it will probably be caused by the pedals, bottom bracket or derailleur pulley (the things that rotate as you pedal), which will need lubrication or replacement.

Hubs

If left unserviced for long periods, the bearings can deteriorate without you knowing it. Loose cones, especially in the rear wheel, can make a racket and will self-destruct pretty quickly – so get them readjusted as soon as possible.

Pedals

Worn cleats are a problem for SPD users. Dry threads in the cranks can also cause creaking. This noise will usually occur when 'standing' on the pedals. Remove the pedals and completely degrease the threads, then apply new grease and retighten.

Handlebars

Constant exposure to wet conditions will create problems with the adjustable elements of the bike (anything that clamps two components together). The water gets in and the residue will 'dry out' and provide problems. Handlebars need to be secured in a smooth stem clamp, so check for burrs and clean out regularly.

Stem

Like the handlebars, problems with the stem are usually down to the clamp 'drying out'. However, the star-fangled nut or a loose top cap can also creak. As with the handlebars, strip and rebuild and check your headset too.

Headset

Dry bearings or broken races will make a very unpleasant creak as you pull on the handlebars. A strip and rebuild will usually eliminate the noise – repack the bearings with grease and fresh bearings if you can. Sometimes the crown race on the fork may need reseating. A knocking sound can mean a loose headset race and may mean the complete unit requires replacement. See pages 124–26 for how to adjust headsets.

Suspension – frame

The frame is usually the cause of noise on suspension bikes. 'Clicking' is a regular fault, and is usually down to dry pivot points or worn DU bushings. Frames with large monocoque frame sections will amplify even the slightest clunk, so it may sound worse than it really is. Spring rear shocks can also rattle loose.

Suspension – fork

Again, any noises are usually down to worn or dried-out bushings. However, be aware of 'hissing' in air forks, as this can mean a leaking seal, or scratching sounds in coil forks, as this can signify a broken spring. Both of these noises will be associated with a loss of performance. Knocking is also a sign of worn bushings, but can also mean that your headset is loose.

Squealing brakes

With V-brakes, this can mean anything of a number of problems (see the V-brake section on pages 69–75 for more information). Most brake noise is down to vibration. Disc brakes will require a regular full clean with a suitable alcohol-based rotor cleaner, and regular replacing of the pads. Check that all the caliper bolts are tight and that the rotor is secured correctly to the hub.

Other problems

Ticking

This usually happens when you pedal and could be caused by:

- the cable hitting the crank or your feet as you pedal
- a loose cassette sprocket
- pedal spindles
- the front derailleur hitting the inside of the right hand crank – you will need to readjust it.

See pages 59–61 for more on front derailleur setup.

Rubbing or whirring from disc brakes

- Whirring usually means that the pads are worn too low.
- Check that the wheels are in straight.
- Recenter the brakes.
- Check whether the rotor is buckled or damaged.

See pages 76–81 for more on disc brake setup.

Chain 'skipping'

- Check the indexing – it should run straight on the sprocket
- If you have crashed recently, the derailleur hanger may well have been bent.

See pages 54–56 for more on rear gear setup.

5

Inner cables and gears

Integrated shifters and nine-speed gears

Shimano invented the indexed gear system (one click, one gear) in the late 1980s. It has evolved over the years and now has 27 gears (nine at the rear wheel and three at the crankset). The latest development is an integrated shifter unit that allows braking and gear changes from one lever, with an additional thumb lever for down shifts. This particular lever is for hydraulic brakes. Derailleur gears can cope with large differences in gear ratios and shift effortlessly through the ratios, so now the whole gear-shifting process is easily done without removing your hands from the handlebars.

GEAR SYSTEMS

SIS (Shimano Index System) is a seven-, eight- or nine-speed setup. A ratchet in the gear lever allows one gear or multiple gears to be shifted with very little effort. One click of the gear lever pulls the cables a preset amount, relative to the distance the derailleur has to move to hop the chain one sprocket on. This is very efficient, but relies on the cable staying put. In time, the cable will stretch and this slight movement throws the whole system out of whack.

Tools required:
· **screwdriver**
· **Teflon lube**

Inner cables

1 To replace the inner gear cable, find the window on the shifter. This is usually a Phillips-head plug. To thread the cable through the window, place the gear shifter in the highest position. You will be able to see the white plastic cable carrier. In this position the cable can be pushed through easily. The screw plug must be replaced after the cable has been threaded through as it prevents muck getting into the system and ruining the mechanism.

2 Gear cables have a smaller nipple than brake cables and they are thinner (1.2 mm). A squirt of Teflon lube on the cable is a good idea, as it will keep the cables loose running.

3 The rear derailleur needs to be installed onto the gear hanger. Check that the hanger is straight and that the threads are clean and uncrossed. The rear gear has to hang perfectly straight. If the hanger is bent or the derailleur cage is twisted, the system will not work.

4 The inner wire is clamped onto the rear derailleur by a washer. To see how this works, look for a channel molded onto the body of the derailleur – the washer will be marked where the cable has been.

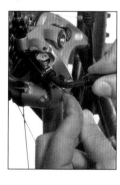

5 Screw the gear barrel adjuster fully in, so that there will be plenty of adjustment available when setting the cable. If all the cable outer sections are properly inserted and the gear shifter is in the highest gear position, it should be possible to pull the cable tight enough with your hand. Pull the cable in the direction of the channel you have identified in step 4. Lock it off with the retaining screw.

6 Rear derailleurs work best with free-running derailleur pulleys. These can be replaced when the plastic wheels wear out. This improves shifting and helps keep the chain in contact with the sprockets on the cassette.

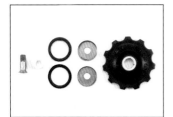

7 To replace the derailleur pulleys, remove the pivot screws. However, if you haven't done this before it's worth paying attention to how it goes back together. Take a photo of the derailleur from both angles if you are in doubt before you remove the bolts. The bushing should be in the center of the wheel.

8 This is the bottom derailleur pulley from a Shimano XT rear derailleur. The bushings are made from a ceramic material so they do not rust up. The top derailleur pulley has a sealed bearing in it. It is worth stripping and reassembling both wheels. Clean them completely and reassemble, using a Teflon lubricant.

9 Make sure that the derailleur pulley is replaced so that it rotates in the right direction. There is usually an arrow on the plastic part of the wheel to help you do this. Once you have reassembled the cage, check that the top and bottom fixing screws are tight.

10 Adjust the limit screw marked 'H' when the chain is in the smallest sprocket (highest gear). It is important that the chain can run smoothly over the sprocket and that the chain cannot move any farther down the block. If this happens, the chain may become trapped between the frame and the cassette and jam up.

11 Next, adjust the limit screw marked 'L' when the gear is in the largest sprocket (lowest gear). Don't worry too much about the indexing working too well at this point, as you need to set the range of the derailleur before tweaking the gears. Double-check that the chain can reach this sprocket, but also that the chain cannot jump over the top of the cassette and into the wheel. Also check that the derailleur cannot hit the spokes of the wheel. This can have disastrous consequences, so it is essential that you make sure this cannot happen.

12 The best way to check your indexing is to hold the back wheel off the ground in a work stand, leaving your hands free to pedal the bike and adjust the cable tension. Start by running through each gear and listening for any noise as you change up the gears, going from the smallest cog to the largest one. Check how easily the chain skips the gears – if it struggles to make the next sprocket then the cable is too loose, so you will need to tighten the cable by screwing the barrel adjuster counter-clockwise. Now change back down the gears (large to small cog) and check if there is a delay in the shift or if the chain stays stuck in one gear – if so, the cable is too tight and you will need to loosen it by turning the adjuster clockwise.

Once the gears are adjusted and working smoothly you need to stretch the cables. Place the gear in the highest position and identify the rear gear cable on the top tube. Tighten the cable clamp to ensure it will not pull through. Grab the inner cable firmly in the center of the open run on the top tube. Pull the cable gently but firmly upward a couple of times. This will seat the outer cables in place and bed the whole cable run into place. Then readjust the gear system as in steps 11 and 12. If the shift is still bad it may be due to one of the following problems:

1. The gear hanger is bent (see pages 145–48 for more on frame preparation).
2. The chain is too long or too short.
3. The cables are old or there is a kink or obstruction somewhere in the run.
4. The chain or sprockets are worn out.
5. The cable is clamped into the rear gear in the wrong place.

Rapid-rise rear derailleurs

Some Shimano gear systems use the rapid-rise system. This is a reverse shifting system and is designed to place less strain on the gears and provide a quicker shift. Adjustment for this system (on XTR) is done at the lever. The principle is exactly the same as above, but I find standard shifting derailleurs easier to adjust with the adjuster set on the drivetrain.

Replacing gear cables

Gear cables are the one element in the gear system that must be friction-free at all times. To keep a smooth-running gear cable you need regular check-ups and plenty of lubrication, and replacing the cables regularly will make your bike shift better and protect the levers from extra wear and tear. The gear cable outer has to be in top condition for the index system to work properly, so always check the cables after crashes as they are very brittle and vulnerable to cracking.

The secret to good-quality cabling is a very good-quality (sharp) set of cable cutters. Only use your cable cutters for cables, not for spokes and small bolts! The easiest way to measure outer cable lengths is to use the old bits of outer cable as cutting templates. The cables should be long enough that they don't snag or pull taut when the handlebars are fully rotated. Over-long cables flap about, which is both inefficient and dangerous.

Tools required:
· **cable cutters**
· **grease**
· **lightweight lubricant**
· **pointed poker or awl (used for making screw holes in wood)**

1 Proper cable cutting is the first step in making your gears work properly. Gear cables have a very brittle plastic outer casing, which can be damaged or cracked by using the wrong cutters when cutting them to length. Use cable shears that slice through the cable rather than pliers or cutters that just crush the casing.

2 The gear cable is different from the brake cable in that it is made up of strands that travel the length of the cable, inside which is a nylon liner that the gear cable can run through. These strands are very hard and cannot be compressed, so they transfer all the effort from the gear shift into bracing the inner cable (or wire). This pulls on the derailleur and in turn pushes the chain onto the next sprocket or chainring.

3 Cutting the outer cable crimps the cable liners, closing up the hole that the inner wire has to go through. Use a poker or an awl to make the hole in the liner big enough for the inner wire to pass through unhindered. This reduces the friction on the cable and enables you to run the inner wires through easily once the cable ferrules are in place.

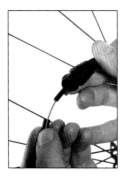

4 Outer cable ferrules must be applied to the end of each cable outer run. Cables without ferrules will fray and crack at the ends and the cracks will travel up the cable, which doesn't do much for your gear shift and allows water to get into the cable. Eventually, the cable strands will push their way through the cable guides and the whole system will pack up. I prefer plastic ferrules as they do not rust and are less likely to seize into the cable guides.

5 Outer gear cable runs should change direction as smoothly as possible. Any tight angles will apply pressure to the inner wire and therefore add friction. This slows the shift and can cause the gears to jump. On suspension bikes it is especially important to make sure that these runs are unhindered and have enough space to move as the bike moves.

6 Apply a small smear of grease to the ferrule before you push it into the cable stop or guide. This will make it easier to adjust the cable at the derailleur and also prevent it from getting stuck or seized up.

7 There is a seal on the final run of cable to the rear derailleur. This is designed to prevent water from running down the cable and into this very sensitive area. Unprotected sections will allow water in and eventually rust the inner wire and dry the outer cable so that the whole thing seizes up.

8 Slotted cable guides enable the cables to be completely separated from the bike. This makes lubrication and inspection of the inner wire easy. To release the cable, place the derailleur in the lowest gear (on the largest sprocket at the back). Then stop pedaling the drive and release the downshift lever completely. This will send the cable completely slack, allowing you to release the cable outers from the guides.

9 The rubber shield shown here covers the adjusting screw on Shimano XT rear derailleurs. It prevents the adjuster from filling up with water and seizing up. You can still adjust the gears with this in place. The final run of outer needs to allow the rear derailleur to travel across all the gears. Allow enough for the gear to be in top and bottom without pulling on the cable or leaving a huge loop of outer.

10 The last run of cable to the rear derailleur is shown here with the rubber covers and weather guards in place. There should be enough cable for the derailleur to move unhindered. Most rear derailleurs pivot around the fixing bolt, so the cable has to be able to move with it. With a short cable problems will arise as you shift into the lower gears, and the shift will be generally tight at the lever.

11 Lastly, remember to protect the frame and the paintwork from the outer cables as vibrations from the trail will cause the cable to wear away at the frame. Place frame stickers where the cables rub, particularly by the handlebars but also at any point where a cable touches the frame. These sticky protectors will protect the cable from wearing through too.

Front derailleur

There are a variety of front derailleur fittings. Derailleurs are essentially guide plates for the chain that allow it to be moved onto the next chainwheel. Most fit to the seat tube with a clamp. However, some Shimano derailleurs fit onto the bottom bracket shell and behind the bracket cups. This type of derailleur is popular on frames that have complicated or interrupted seat tubes – usually on suspension bikes.

Tools required:
- **small Phillips-head screwdriver**
- **5 mm Allen keys**

Shimano has perfected this mechanism to be 'indexed', so now one click at the lever allows for one chainring shift at the cranks. At least, that's the theory. Using the front derailleur properly takes practice, and you can only do this if it has been set up well in the first place. Setting it up also takes time and practice. It's a very dynamic mechanism so it does require patience to get it perfect. Height, angle and throw are all influencing factors.

The plates are shaped so that they will not rub on the chain when they are set correctly, and so that they can pick up the chain and carry it to the next chainring. For many mechanics, the front derailleur is their biggest headache.

Installing and adjusting the front derailleur

1 Angle the derailleur so that it is exactly parallel with all three chainrings. When you buy a new front derailleur it should have a small plastic spacer inside the mechanism. Do not pull this out as it is there to help you set the position and height of the derailleur. It allows you to align the outside plate of the derailleur with the outer (biggest) chainring and position the derailleur over the middle chainring. If you can't get the derailleur into this position, you may have problems with the chainline and you may need a different length bottom bracket.

2 If the angle is slightly out (as shown here), the shifting will be sloppy, so make sure you set the angle carefully. Spend time getting this bit right as it will have the biggest influence on the performance of the derailleur. If it is angled too far outward it will rub on the crank when the pedals are turned.

3 The distance between the outside derailleur plate and the teeth of the chainring should be no more than 2–3 mm. This will ensure that the derailleur is correctly positioned to cope with the difference in size of the granny (smallest) ring and big ring. It also allows for the chain pick-up and will happily clear the teeth of the chainrings.

4 A good chainline is imperative; make sure that the chain can access all of the rear sprockets when in the middle chainring. You can also see that the derailleur in this position is exactly in line with the outer (big) chainring.

5 This full suspension bike needs a higher fitting derailleur (the clamp is farther up the seat tube). However, the steps for adjusting it remain the same, and the space between the cage plate and the chainring is identical.

6 Next, attach the gear cable. Make sure that the gear shifter is in its lowest position so the cable is at its slackest. In this position the front derailleur will be over the granny ring. Pull the cable through the clamp firmly. Trap the cable in the clamp and check that it's in the right place, as this can affect the shift. Once the cable is pulled through and set you can adjust the low-limit stop screw.

7 Adjust the limit screw marked 'L' first. Place the rear derailleur in the biggest sprocket (lowest/easiest gear), as this is the farthest the chain will travel. Then set the front derailleur so it only just clears the inside of the plate. In the granny ring you will probably only use three or four of the lowest gears; make sure these work properly and then shift into the biggest chainring.

8 Now you can adjust the limit screw marked 'H'. Put the chain onto the big chainring (this may over-shift at first) and work the rear derailleur through all the gears. You will notice that the chain changes angle considerably, but it will cope with most of the gears on this chainring. Set the limit screw so that in the smallest rear sprocket it just clears the chain.

9 On a full suspension bike this adjustment can be very tricky. Here the swing arm is in the way of the adjustment screws, so you would need to use a longer screwdriver. However, you can see that the plate of the front derailleur is set so that the chain is not rubbing even in the largest size sprocket at the rear.

Causes of front derailleur rubbing

If your front derailleur is rubbing, it will be due to one of the following problems:

1. The cable is too tight or too loose.
2. The limit screws are incorrectly adjusted.
3. The angle of the derailleur angle to the chainrings is wrong.
4. The chainline is incorrect.

Causes of derailing a chain

If you have problems with the chain coming off, it will be caused by one of the following:

1. The low adjust is set incorrectly, so you will have to push the derailleur farther out with the limit screw.
2. The chain is jumping over the top of the biggest chainring, so you will need to push the derailleur farther in with the limit screw.

TIP

A plastic tire lever jammed (carefully) into the parallelogram mechanism can simulate the 'setup' spacer and will also allow you two hands to adjust the fastening bolt and the derailleur angle.

Top or bottom pull?

Most mountain bikes use a top-pull front derailleur. However, some frame designs necessitate the use of a bottom-pull mechanism. Most quality front derailleurs have a swappable option so that you can use either system on the same derailleur.

top   bottom

SRAM shifters and derailleurs

Gripshifters has been a viable alternative to Shimano for well over ten years. Now known as SRAM, the company makes a wide range of shifters and gear mechanisms for use with pretty much all makes of mountain bike gear systems. SRAM can be used with either a Shimano HG or SRAM chains and either Shimano or SRAM ESP rear derailleurs. SRAM gear systems will handle cassette ratios of 11:28 to 14:34 and chainring combinations of 22/32/42, 24/34/46 and 26/36/46 or 48.

The main difference between Shimano and SRAM rear derailleurs is that SRAM cannot use the sprung-pivot fixing bolt that Shimano can. This is at the bolt and gives you the advantage of a mechanism that moves as you shift between the chainrings. It's no better or worse than Shimano, just different.

Tools required:
- pointed awl or small screwdriver
- Allen key
- cable cutters
- pliers

Gripshift

SRAM's Gripshift system is a viable alternative to Shimano gears. The twist-grip gear shifter is simple and easy to service, and many cross-country racers prefer this system for its light weight and simple operation. Their 1:1 gearshift ratio makes the action very light and precise. Now SRAM have made trigger shifters and front derailleurs so you can have a non-Shimano-equipped bike with the disc brake of your choice. For the mechanic, the main advantage of this system is that Gripshift shifters are very simple to service and can easily be rebuilt.

1 Fit the Gripshifter so that there is plenty of room for grips and bar ends. Be careful not to overtighten the fixing bolts as they can break the fixing clamp very easily. Also, be careful not to jam the gear adjuster behind the brake lever – position it so that it is protected from impact by the brake lever housing.

2 Gear cable replacement is relatively straightforward with all Gripshift shifters. First, place the gear selector in the highest gear (marked 7, 8 or 9 depending on how many gears you have) and pick out the rubber cover plate from the body of the shifter to reveal the nipple at the end of the gear cable.

3 The gear cable nipple is trapped behind a retaining plate and will need to be poked out with a pointed awl or small screwdriver. You may have to jiggle the twist grip a little to persuade it to come out.

4 SRAM's paddle-type shifters are similar in fitting to Shimano. They have Allen bolts sensibly placed on the top of the handlebar, which makes them very easy to install and adjust. Position them tight up behind the brake lever, but be careful not to obstruct the barrel adjuster.

5 Measure and cut a length of cable for the front shifter and the rear derailleur. Unlike Shimano, SRAM rear derailleurs do not pivot with a spring at the fixing bolt, so getting the cable length exactly right is critical. The cable enters the derailleur from the front and doesn't encounter the same friction problems as Shimano's more 'looped' piece of gear cable. Check the manufacturer's instructions for recommended lengths, and see pages 57–58 for more on fitting cables.

6 Adjust the limit screw marked 'H' for the highest gear setting to align the top pulley (or jockey) wheel with the outside edge of the smallest sprocket.

7 Then adjust the setting marked 'L'. However, this time align the top jockey wheel with the dead center of the largest sprocket. Check that the derailleur cannot hit the spokes.

8 Now you can install the chain and place the derailleur in the smallest cog and granny (smallest) chainring. In this position, adjust the chain gap with the screw at the back of the derailleur – the distance between the top pulley and the sprocket should be 6 mm.

9 Pull the cable tight with a pair of pliers as you fix it in place. As with Shimano, do this in the highest gear setting on the shifter and check that the adjuster is wound in to allow more room for adjustment.

10 Pull the cable through the rear cable run and over the fin at the back of the derailleur, and attach it in the correct side of the fixing bolt. Then run through the gears and reset the chain gap if necessary (it should be 6 mm away from all the sprockets).

Like Shimano XTR rapid-rise mechanisms, the adjustment for SRAM shifters and gears can only be done at the lever. However, the process is exactly the same (see pages 54–56 for more on cables and indexing). Stretch the cables to check they are bedded in, and readjust them if necessary. Run through the gears again and recheck the chain gap.

SRAM TIPS

- As with all gear mechanisms, you will need to pull up the slack as you tighten the gear inner wire. Unlike Shimano, there are several options of SRAM shifter. In the instructions you will see that there are different fixing points for different gear setups and shifters.
- To get the correct chain length, measure the chain so that it is tight when placed from biggest sprocket to biggest chainring, bypassing the rear derailleur (do this before it is attached), then add two links.
- As with Shimano derailleurs, strip and rebuild the derailleur pulleys after muddy rides and long periods of wet weather. Lubricate the parallelogram mechanism with a light Teflon-based lube.
- Cable length is key to rear shifting success, so make sure you get this right. Once installed, regular cleaning and lubrication of the cable will help keep the shift crisp. Always keep the cable fin at the back of the derailleur clean and free of grit.

Chains – replacement and care

Chains are designed to wear out. They are incredibly efficient, but have to put up with a lot of abuse, and the constant twisting and shifting up and down the sprockets wears the average mountain bike chain out in a matter of months.

A combination of good gear technique, constant chainline and regular care will prolong a chain's life. Look at a singlespeed bike – chains that don't move from side to side will last years rather than months.

There is also a variety of quality of chain. Plated chains are the best, as they are less likely to corrode and therefore last longer and shift better than a plain steel chain. Stainless steel chains are also available; they last a little longer than plain steel chains but, as they are harder, they can wear aluminum chainrings if they aren't regularly cleaned and lubricated.

Replacing an old, worn-out chain usually requires replacing the cassette as well; as the chain stretches, it wears the cassette sprockets too, making the whole drivetrain scrap. This can be expensive, so using a cheap chain and replacing it often – rather than buying an expensive chain and waiting until it wears out the sprockets and chainring too – will turn out cheaper in the long run.

Tools required:
. **chain checker or ruler**
. **quality chain tool**
. **pliers**
. **grease**

1 Measure across 24 links of the chain – it should measure 12 inches. If it's more than that, the chain has stretched beyond a usable length. A chain in this state will start to wear other components and shifting will become increasingly erratic.

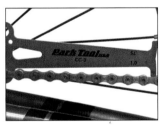

2 There are several chain-measuring devices, but the Park one pictured here is the best value one on the market. Simply hook one end into the link and use either side to ascertain how much stretch there is in the links. In this case, the gauge will not slot into the corresponding link as the chain is brand new.

3 This method shows you very quickly the state of the chain and the chainrings. Put the chain on the biggest chainring and smallest cassette sprocket. If you can pull the chain off the chainring and it can clear the tip of one of the chainring teeth, or the chain moves excessively at the top and bottom of the chainwheel (demonstrated here at the front derailleur and crank arm), there is some chain wear and it should be replaced.

4 When a mountain bike chain is at its correct length, the rear derailleur cage should be exactly vertical when the gear is placed in the highest combination (big chainring and small sprocket). If you are replacing a chain, check that this is the case before you remove the old chain.

5 This is the biggest spread of sprocket to chainring that is possible. You can see that the chain is pulling the rear derailleur at a very extreme angle. Some mechanics use this position to measure the chain, placing the chain in this ratio so that it is tight and adding two links to allow for the derailleur.

6 At the other end of the gear range you will only need a few of the lowest gears. Check that these can be reached easily and that the top derailleur pulley doesn't rub on the largest cassette sprocket.

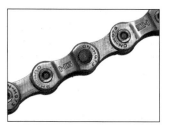

7 This flat-ended pin marks the spot where the chain was first joined. Find this link and break the chain exactly opposite it. Remove the old chain and measure the new one next to it. Depending on the type of chain, you will have to remove a few links from one end. The chain is made up of side plates and links with rollers inside them to assist in the smooth running of the gearing and pedal action.

8 Thread the new chain through the rear derailleur pulleys and over the chainwheel. Don't put it back on the chainring until you have joined the chain, as the slack will make it easier to rejoin the two ends. The Shimano chain is joined with this special pin. It has a narrow, pointed part to make sure that the link is pushed in the correct way. I cover the pin with some grease so that it will go in easily; this also means that it's less likely to push the plates out of shape as it goes through the link.

9 Push the link through using a quality Shimano-chain-compatible chain-rivet tool. This Park tool has shaped jaws to prevent the side plates becoming squeezed together. Keep the chain straight and turn the handle firmly and slowly to make sure that the pin goes through straight.

10 The Park chain tool is set up so that it stops once the link is in place (there is a circlip on the threaded shaft that prevents you going too far). There is a definite click as the pin passes through the link. When you reach this point, back off the handle and check that the pin is in place.

11 When the Shimano pin is through to the other side and the fatter part of the pin is equally spaced on either side of the link plates, snap off the guide with some pliers. Obviously, you need to do this before you check the gears are working.

12 Once the pin is in place there may be a little stiffness in the link, which may jump as you pedal the gears backward. To remove a stiff link, first add some lube to it and push it into an inverted V shape. Then place your thumbs on the links to either side of this link. Grip the chain and *gently* push the chain against itself. This very careful 'bending' should free the link immediately.

SRAM chains

SRAM chains come with 'quick-release' links called Power Links. They can fix a chain without the need for tools and are really handy to use on the trail for emergencies – so carry one in your trail tool kit. They are easy to install and save you messing about with chain tools every time you want to take a chain off.

To remove them, simply take the tension off the chain (I find it best to take the chain off the chainrings first) and push the links against each other and your hands toward one another at the same time. It takes practice, but is a great way to remove your chain for washing.

Fitting them requires removing the side plates from both ends of the chain so they join the chain between two rollers.

CHAIN TIPS

· For the best results, replace your chain every 1,200–1,800 miles. This will prevent wear to the cassette sprockets, chain rings and derailleurs.

· Swap steel rings for aluminum ones and replace them at least every one to two years.
If you want to experiment with chain lengths, do so with an old chain and decide on the final length before you cut a new one.

· Buy a chain bath and clean your chain once a week.

· Degrease and thoroughly clean a new chain before using it. They are packed in grease for storage to stop them from rusting, but this just attracts trail dirt the minute you head off-road. Run the chain through a chain bath and relube with a quality chain lube to keep your new chain clean for longer.

· A chain 'jumps' when there is something worn in the drivetrain. Usually, if you fit a new chain it will skip over the cassette sprockets in some ratios, which means that the cassette needs replacing too. However, a new chain can sometimes jump on just the middle chainring, and usually in all the gears on the cassette, when there is less chain tension from the rear derailleur. You can solve this by replacing the chainring.

· Chain suck usually happens when you shift to extreme gear ratios for climbing and are placing a lot of pressure on the pedals. This gets worse as the chain wears out. Hooked and worn chainrings also affect chain suck as the chain 'sticks' to the chainrings and gets jammed between the frame and the chainset. The best solution is to keep components clean and replace them often, before chain suck happens.

6

V-brakes

Fitting and servicing V-brakes

The V-brake is the most powerful cable-activated rim-brake design. It can provide a variety of setup problems, and care is needed when adjusting them.

Servicing your V-brakes on a regular basis is essential – they have to be looked after carefully if you want to get the best performance from them. Regularly removing the brakes from the bike and thoroughly cleaning all the parts (using an old toothbrush to clean the mechanism) will keep them smooth. Lubricate all the pivots with a dry lube, taking care not to contaminate the pads, and make sure there is no rust on the steel parts. V-brakes are

BRAKING SYSTEMS

particularly sensitive to water and can seize up if neglected for long periods. So, as with most components on a mountain bike, they need to be prepared properly.

It's important to use the correct, V-brake-compatible brake lever. Using the wrong lever (with too much leverage) can be very dangerous; the V-brake lever is designed to provide the right amount of leverage with two-finger braking. The position of the gear cable nipple in relation to the pivot point and the amount of cable that it pulls in one squeeze are critical.

Tools required:

. **emery cloth**
. **grease**
. **5 mm Allen key**
. **needle nose pliers**
. **torque wrench**

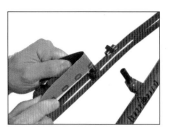

1 Prepare the cantilever studs (otherwise known as canti-studs or sometimes brake bosses) on the frame. If they are rusty, or if the brakes are a little rough and notchy in their action, you may need to clean off the stud with some emery cloth. Use a thin strip of a fine grade so that the finish is smooth.

2 Grease the faces of the canti-stud, as it acts as a pivot for the brake; however, some better quality brakes have their own bearing inside the brake. Some brakes have a brass sleeve that fits snugly over the canti-stud – this is the bushing that the brake pivots on. Greasing this and checking it regularly will also prevent the stud from rusting up and the brake sticking or seizing onto the bike.

3 The frame, or fork, canti-stud will have up to three small holes in it on the inside of the stud (in this case there is only one hole). These holes retain the stopper pin on the back of the brake, securing the brake and enabling the spring to act against the brake lever to return the brake to the open position. On cantilever brakes, this can be used to put more return spring into the action. All V-brakes should be used with the one centrally positioned hole.

4 The fixing bolts have a locking compound that prevents them vibrating loose under braking forces. I would suggest squirting a little thin oil into the canti-stud, especially if you have had to retap the threads. This will prevent the threads from rusting up. Copper slip is also good for this as it is very hard to wash away.

5 Finally, tighten the fixing bolts to around 7 Nm using a torque wrench. This will need to be rechecked once in a while as vibrations can shake the bolts loose. You can replace these bolts with longer stainless steel ones (and Loctite them in) if you want long-term reliability.

6 The pads are curved to follow the shape of the rim. Make sure that the pads are set just below the top of the rim (about 2 mm), but the pads should also be flat in order to act upon all the braking surface of the rim. Also check that the pads are facing in the right direction and are on the correct caliper arm (usually marked left and right on the brake pad).

Adjusting V-brake blocks

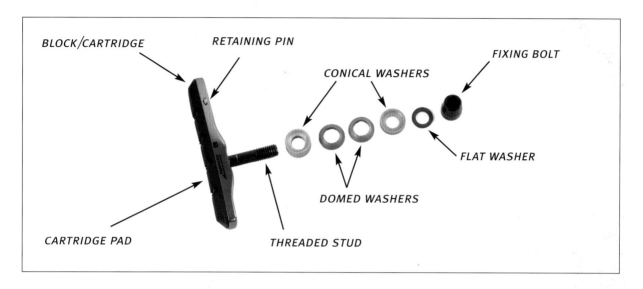

BLOCK/CARTRIDGE   RETAINING PIN   CONICAL WASHERS   FIXING BOLT

FLAT WASHER

DOMED WASHERS

CARTRIDGE PAD   THREADED STUD

1 The pad is fully adjustable for angle as the retaining washers and spacers act as a ball joint, which allows the pad to be moved to hit the rim from any angle. Make sure that the wheel is centered in the bike before you start to adjust the pad angle as this can make a big difference.

2 First of all, loosely fit the pads to the rim so you can have a look at the setup. The distance between the noodle-retaining cage and the fastening bolt should be over 39 mm. This distance will be influenced by the rim width and the position of the canti-studs, but you can tweak it by replacing the concave spacers and domed washers to move the arms away from the rim.

3 The best way to adjust the pad angle is to hold the pad in place with one hand and the Allen key in the other. Make small adjustments and always keep the pads symmetrical. If the pads are hard to adjust or will not stay in place, check that the domed washers are installed correctly. Once the pads are set you can check they don't rotate in your fingers and set the nuts to 9–10 Nm.

4 There is some 'toe-in' set on the pads, which allows them to be 'sucked in' toward the rim as the brake is applied. Set the cables so that there is a gap of about 1–2 mm on either side of the rim, then adjust the spring tension screw to pull the brake central (see step 6 on page 70). In this position the toe-in should be no more than 1 mm from front to back.

5 Once you are happy that the pads are tight and set at the correct angle and height you can center the brake properly. This will affect how the brake feels at the lever, so check that is still feels easy to apply the brakes. Give the brake a few hard pulls to check that it returns and that the wheel can spin without rubbing

Removing cartridge-type pads

The best type of pad is one that allows you to replace the rubber part only and has an aluminum backing that stays in place. This 'cartridge' system only needs setting up once and you can change pads quickly.

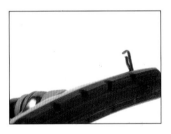

1 Once the brake shoe is in place, pad replacement is simple as the only part that has to be moved is the pad. Pull out the split pin from the top of the shoe (you may need to push it up from the bottom and catch hold of it with a pair of needle-nose pliers). It is likely that the pin will be bent or dropped on the floor, so it's best to replace the pin too. All good-quality replacement pads will come with a pair of spare pins.

2 Slide the pad out of the shoe – pads tend to be quite loose fitting so this should be easy. Replace the pad and make sure you are using the correct pad (they are usually marked left and right). If you are in doubt, look for the channel in the back of the pad where the split pin slots through and secures it to the shoe.

3 The pin must be inserted so that it is visible on either side of the shoe. You will know that it is properly installed as it will be easy to push all the way through. If it won't go in easily, slide the pad back and forth a little until the pin 'pops' into place. The spring in the pin retains the pad, making sure it doesn't drop out.

V-brake cable replacement

You should check for cable trouble on a regular basis and always take care of your cables when releasing the brakes to remove the wheels, as they are vulnerable and susceptible to kinking. Kinked cables and water inside the outers will slow your braking down considerably. It's hard to tell when the inner wire is kinked but a sloppy or stiff feeling in the lever action is a dead give-away. Replacing the cable run is the best way to solve this, but stripping out the inner and using a quality spray lube can be a short-term fix.

It's pretty rare for a brake cable to fray dangerously, but it's worth checking the inner cable, especially if the brakes are feeling stiffer than usual. This friction can be caused by the inner cable rubbing on either a burr on the outer cable or a frame cable stop. It's also rare for cables to snap, but they can fray at the clamp bolts which can make future adjustment difficult.

You can adjust cable tension at the levers 'on the fly' using the adjusters on the lever at the handlebar. Simply unscrew the center section and the inner cable will tighten. Then lock it off with the outer lock ring. Check the lever a few times and make sure you have left enough play for the wheel to spin freely. We ran through lever reach in 'Basic bike setup' on pages 19–21. However, adjusting the reach can affect the pull of the brake lever, so long-term adjustment of the slack in a cable system is best done by pulling the cable through at the brake-cable fastening bolt on the caliper.

BRAKING TIPS

- Ceramic rims are a great idea for V-brakes if you are having trouble stopping. They do require special pads, as standard rubber pads can wreck the surface, glazing it up and making it unusable.
- Clean rims will make a huge difference to brake performance. Use disc-brake cleaner to clean your rims and regularly remove all the grime that builds up, as brake dust will just act as an abrasive and wear down both the rim and the pads.
- Squealing is caused by vibration. As the pad hits the rim it applies friction to slow the wheel down. The result of this friction is vibration and a buildup of heat. This wears down the brake pads and can also create a hell of a racket. Toe in the pads and you'll alleviate the problem. However, if this still doesn't work there may be excessive play in the brake assembly and it may need to be replaced.
- V-brake pads wear fairly evenly and slowly in the dry. However, in the wet you can wear through a set in a matter of hours, especially if it's muddy. As V-brake pads are usually very low profile, they wear out in a matter of months in the summer and weeks in the winter. If you want razor-sharp braking from V-brakes, fit some ceramic rims and ceramic-compatible pads.
- Over-long cables will usually add friction and absorb braking power, so keep the cable lengths to a minimum without sacrificing movement in the handlebars and suspension systems. You should replace the nylon noodle insert if it is damaged, and oil and replace cables regularly.
- Braking can be improved at the lever by adjusting the lever pull. Many brake levers have adjustable cable positions to offer more or less leverage from the lever. The more leverage you have, the sharper the brake will be. Avid levers have a special knob, which can be dialed by hand. Shimano V-brake levers have either an adjustment knob or a plastic block that can be removed. This can make the brakes sharper, so test-ride the bike before you try anything too extreme.

1 Cables can be removed quickly by turning the adjustment screw on the lever so that the slot faces forward and lines up with the slot in the brake lever body. Release the brakes at the calipers and then pull gently on the lever. As you release the lever, the cable will slacken and the inner cable can be fed through this slot. See page 22 for more on unhooking V-brakes.

2 The nipple can then be unhooked from the lever. Be careful when you return the cables and make sure that the cables are properly relocated into the adjusters, noodles and frame stops, so that they cannot slip out when the brake is applied.

3 Mountain bike brake cables have a barrel nipple that rotates slightly in the lever every time you pull on the brakes. Greasing the nipple will prevent friction and stop any noises developing as the levers are applied. Inspect the nipples regularly and check for any signs of wear and tear on the cable around the nipple.

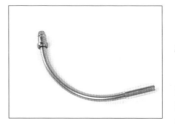

4 The cable 'noodle' pipe comes in two lengths. The shorter (90-degree) one is for the rear brakes and the longer (170-degree) one is for the front brakes. This is to make sure that the brakes can be released time after time without damaging the inner or outer cables. See page 22 for information on how to release cable noodles.

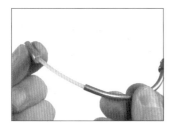

5 The 'noodle' pipe has a nylon insert that provides protection for the cable and also helps prevent friction in this part of the cable run. When new these pipes have a small amount of grease squirted into them and it's a good idea to check regularly that the cable is still well lubricated. Use a very small amount of waterproof grease and inject it with a grease gun.

6 Cables should be measured (it's easiest to use the old cables as a template) and cut using a quality cable cutter. Make sure that the ends of the cable are flat – they can be tidied up with a metal file – and that the inner nylon part is open at the ends.

7 Unlike gear cables, it is only necessary to add a ferrule where the cable will contact the frame stops. The V-brake noodle has its own built-in ferrule. New brake cables usually have a factory-fitted ferrule on one end – I always start with this one at the lever adjuster.

8 The rear brake cable must be precision-cut so that the curve of the cable is unhindered and smooth. Over-long cables flap about and create friction and can also catch passing undergrowth. However, short cables will pull on the calipers and potentially decentralize them over the rims.

9 Cable doughnuts are used to prevent the cable slapping on the top tube and wearing out the paintwork (the noise of flapping cables is also highly annoying!). Some people use plastic sleeves instead; however, quality cables are usually made from stainless steel and do not have to be covered, while plastic sleeves can help retain moisture, which will eventually corrode the cables.

10 The gaiter covers the cable as it exits the noodle and prevents any water and mud getting into the noodle pipe. They are not essential and the brake will work perfectly well without them. However, the noodle is the weak link in the V-brake system and needs constant care. It's always worth stripping and relubricating the noodle after wet rides.

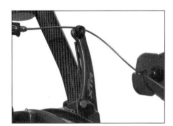

11 Thread the cable through the fixing bolt and pull the calipers together with the cable. Fasten the inner cable into the caliper using a 5 mm Allen key. Leave 50–60 mm of cable to allow for further adjustment and cut the cable with a sharp cable cutter.

12 Lastly, add a cable-end cap to prevent the cable from fraying. This will prevent injury and enable you to make further adjustments to the brakes.

Cable-activated disc brakes

Many entry- and mid-range mountain bikes come with cable discs and, if you set them up properly and maintain them well, they can be just as effective as hydraulic brakes. They also mean you can start off with efficient brakes for less initial outlay. You can use your bike's existing cable brake levers and cable guides, which can be neater. Like hydraulics, cable discs are far easier to look after than V-brakes or cantilevers, and they work much better in the mud. Cable discs can also be serviced without having to buy hydraulic oils and getting messy, so in some situations (such as world tours or adventure rides) it will be a lot more convenient to carry spares and readjust the brakes if you have a cable set-up.

As the cable is an integral part of the brake, you need to follow the same rules for cable management and care as you would for V-brakes (see pages 73–75). Looking after your cables and replacing them regularly will keep your brakes feeling as good as new.

Shimano and Avid discs are very similar in design. They use a lever that activates a helicoil plunger, which in turn presses the pad onto the disc.

All cable disc systems are very simple to set up, especially if you follow the rules below.

Tools required:
- **torque (star-shaped) key**
- **torque wrench**
- **Loctite (refer to manufacturer's recommendations)**
- **long (needle-nose) pliers**
- **cable pullers (optional)**

Disc brakes

Disc brakes sound (and look) complicated, but high-quality disc brake systems are the easiest things to set up and service. There is a variety of different standards for fitting to your bike and there is also a range of hub systems. Hydraulic disc brakes are now lightweight and incredibly efficient, and are sealed to the elements so will always give you predictable, sharp braking. The cables don't need constant attention after wet rides and the calipers also require little readjustment once they have been set up. Disc brakes are getting lighter too, so all riders – from downhill to cross-country – will be using them before too long.

1 Fit the disc rotors to the hubs. These Shimano rotors have washers that are designed to secure the bolt and prevent it from undoing completely. Many trucks have a similar device to keep their wheel bolts in check. Also check that the rotor direction arrows are pointing in the direction of rotation. You should check that these bolts are tight on a regular basis. Use some Loctite on the bolts if you remove or replace the discs, as undoing the bolt will damage the thread lock.

2 Tighten the rotor bolts to 4 Nm. Turn the bolts a quarter-turn only at a time, working gradually on opposite or alternate bolts until you reach the desired torque setting. Do not tighten up one bolt completely and then the next, as doing these bolts up unevenly and can distort the rotor.

3 Once the rotor is in place you can 'set' the washers by bending them to sit flat with the head of the rotor bolt, which is three-sided. This is an added precaution that prevents the bolts from vibrating loose. Once the disc is installed, leave it for a few hours before you ride to give the Loctite a chance to set properly.

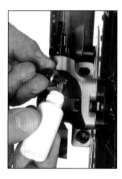

4 Secure the brake caliper to the fork or frame. There are several adapters available depending on what type of fork or rotor size you have. Add some Loctite to the bolts and tighten them to make them secure. It is important to realize that tightening each bolt equally and to the right torque setting is far more important than just doing them up as tight as you can. The Loctite is for additional safety and to prevent the bolts from vibrating loose.

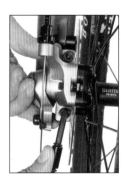

5 The caliper on Shimano and Avid brakes is very easy to adjust – you simply center the disc pads over the rotor. The caliper is mounted on slotted bolt-holes, which allow a fair bit of side-to-side movement; this means that this type of caliper can be fitted to forks or frames that do not have perfectly aligned brake bosses. However, it is still a good idea to have the brake bosses faced.

6 Pull the cable through the caliper with either a pair of pliers or a cable puller. This will make sure that the cable is in the correct position and that the slack is out of the lever.

7 Tighten the Allen key bolt on the brake caliper to 7 Nm. Although this bolt needs to be tight enough to prevent the cable from slipping through the clamp, if it is too tight it can crush and damage the cable, causing it to fray around the clamp. Once the cable is attached, you can stretch the cables and double-check the cable tension.

8 To 'bed' the cables in and stretch the system, pull hard on the brake lever several times. This will also check you have done the bolts up tightly enough. Repeat steps 6 and 7 if the cable has slipped at all, or if there is excessive movement in the lever. You can then set the cable tension perfectly by using the adjusting screw on either the brake lever or the caliper, as shown here. You may have to run through steps 6 and 7 again to make sure that the cable is correctly secured and tensioned.

9 The throw of the disc caliper can be fine-tuned using the adjustment screw on the back of the caliper unit. Avid has a red button to twist for this adjustment. Be careful to check that the throw is tuned as the pads wear; this will ensure progressive pad wear and braking effectiveness. Check all the bolts on the caliper regularly as they can vibrate loose over time.

10 Finally, check all the torque settings on the rotor bolts and calipers and test the brakes before you ride. Bed the pads in so that they don't glaze up. Make sure that the cables are all tidy – you can use electrical ties to keep the cables out of the way. Check that the cables can't get caught in the suspension forks as you steer, and bounce the forks up and down a few times to check they can't snag on the cables. See pages 79–81 for more on pad replacement and care.

TIPS

- The procedure for disc replacement is the same for most disc systems. However, some retaining pins can have a split pin on the end to stop the pin from vibrating loose. If this is the case on your bike, remember to remove the split pin before you undo the retaining pin.
- The pad pin can, in some cases, be threaded. In this case, undo the retaining pin and pull it out carefully using needle-nose pliers. Do not pull too hard as you can damage the threads inside the caliper. See pages 79–81 for more on pad replacement and care.
- To center the brakes quickly with the cable already installed, undo both of the angle-adjusting bolts. Pull the brake into the full-on position and tie a toe strap or zip tie around the brake to hold it in place. Tighten the angle bolts with the brake applied. Undo the tie and spin the wheel, which should be spot-on. Then tweak the pad alignment.

Replacing pads

Fitting new disc calipers does take time to get right. However, if you use the recommended rotors, hubs and levers, they will work far better. Once they have been set up correctly, replacing disc pads is really easy.

The calipers for the front and rear brakes are different sizes, so make sure you have the correct caliper before you start. There are two types of disc caliper fixing systems too – ISO two-bolt and pillar-mounted (the latter are used on Manitou forks and some Shimano brakes). Rotors also come in a variety of sizes depending on the system you are using.

Tools required:
- torque wrench
- brake-mount facing tool (Hope or Magura)
- Allen keys
- disc-brake cleaner
- needle-nose pliers
- grease

Types of pad

Organic pads
Once fitted, organic compound pads need 'breaking in' before you ride them properly off-road. To do this, find a hill and do twenty firm 'stops' from about 12–18 m/h. This stabilizes the compound and prevents the pads from disintegrating under pressure or wearing quickly. A word of warning – do not coast the brakes until you have broken them in to avoid 'cooking' the pads.

Sintered pads
Sintered pads don't need to be broken in. They are very slightly heavier and get hotter than organic compound pads and therefore shouldn't be used in some brake systems (such as Magura), so always read the instructions! Sintered pads work very well, but they do wear the rotor out more quickly than organic-type pads.

Mixing pads and pad wear
Some riders experiment with mixing different types of pads in the calipers to alter brake feel and performance. Obviously, the disc pad is hidden so you can't check for pad wear easily, but if you are taking the wheels out of the bike always check to see how much wear is left in the pads. Once the pad has worn out, you risk brake failure and a nasty accident should the base of the pad catch on the rotor.

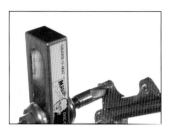

1 Most disc brake problems are due to uneven mounting. Most frame mounts are slightly out of whack (welding around the dropouts can distort them). Have your frame checked out using Magura's 'Gnann-o-mat' (named after the German man who invented it, Herr Gnann); this tool will remove any extra material from shaky bosses, placing the caliper in line with the rotor and the hub.

2 The calipers must be centered over the rotor, rather than over the pads themselves, to make sure that the pads wear evenly and to prevent vibration and any nasty noises. Make sure that the wheel is tight in the frame – if it isn't, it can slightly affect the final rotor and caliper positions.

3 To fine-tune the spacing between the pad and the rotor you can add shims to the mount on either the fork or the frame. These are available in a variety of sizes (0.2 mm, 1 mm, 2 mm and 3 mm). A little grease on the shims will stick them together and help you hold onto them as you thread the bolts through the caliper. This can be very tricky!

4 Once you're happy that the rotor is centered in the caliper and the faces are square, tighten the fixing bolts. Refer to the manufacturer's recommended torque settings. As a general guide, the setting will usually be 6 Nm, which is not as tight as you'd expect. Once the bolt is tight, you may find that the pads drag on the rotor, so you will have to readjust it until there is no drag. This can take a while to get just right, but it's worth getting this right so take your time.

5 Shimano XTR and XT discs have a threaded pin with a split pin on one end to retain the bolt should it start to shake loose. If this pin pops out, you can expect brake failure and a potentially nasty accident, as the cylinders inside the caliper can come out if the pads fall out. Fluid will also spray everywhere and ruin your bike – so make sure that these pins are returned correctly!

6 Hayes pads use a retaining spring rather than a magnet to secure the pad to the top of the cylinder. This is very easy to locate and snaps in and out instantly. Make sure the pads are properly replaced before returning the wheel; if you have trouble getting the disc in, you haven't clipped the pads in properly.

7 Pads that use a split pin rather than a retaining spring need careful attention. Once you have straightened out the splayed ends using a pair of needle-nose pliers, you can pull the pin out.

8 When you have removed the split pin, squeeze the pads together and pull them out of the caliper. You can then clean the caliper with disc brake cleaner and inspect the cylinders inside the caliper for any leaks or wear.

9 These Shimano pads have a leaf spring in between the two pads. The spring is easy to replace as it has a hole in the top of it that matches up with either side of the caliper and the pads. Return the new pads and replace the split pin. Make sure the split pin is properly secured.

10 Whatever system you have, it's always worth checking that the caliper hasn't moved since you last replaced the pads. This type of post-mounted rear caliper is very simple to center as it is mounted on slotted bolt-holes.

11 Finally, thoroughly clean the brake rotor with rotor cleaner. Do not use a water-repelling spray lube or anything with oil in it. The pads contaminate very easily and the smallest amount of grease (even hamburger fat!) can ruin a new set of pads.

Rotor wear

Rotors do wear out eventually. However, they last a lot longer if you refresh your pads regularly and keep the calipers and rotors clean. Just like rims, rotors can buckle, usually due to excessive heat build up or lack of care when throwing them into the back of the car. If this happens, your brakes will drag and slow you down. Remember that the rotor-to-pad spacing is around 0.5 mm so it won't take much of a buckle to mess it all up, not to mention wear pads out faster and provide irregular performance. Change the rotors if they are damaged to keep your brakes safe.

Rotor performance

Wavy rotors are becoming more popular. They keep the pads slightly cooler than standard round rotors and prevent the heat that builds up in the pistons from cooking the brake fluid. This build up can have a dramatic effect on brake performance and make the brakes fade under pressure on long down-hills. Wavy discs also 'shave' the pads and thus prevent the glaze on the pad from building up. The result is faster pad wear but more efficient braking per-formance.

Quick-release levers

On all disc brake systems make sure that you use a good-quality quick-release lever, preferably made of steel – Shimano quick releases are particu-larly good. Then tighten the lever firmly and check it regularly. See pages 32–34 for more on removing wheels and using a quick-release lever.

The Shimano center lock is set to be the industry standard for disc brake fitting. Most hub manufacturers offer a center lock option, which is a ser-rated spline fitting for the rotor attached to the hub using a cassette lockring-style tool. It is far easier to fit than the six-bolt fitting and is also safer, as long as it is tightened to the correct torque setting.

Hydraulic disc brakes

Hydraulic disc brakes terrify most home mechanics, but the truth is they are possibly the easiest thing to set up and service. They have the advantage over rim brakes in that once they are set up properly, they need little effort to retain consistent and predictable braking, and they are far better than a cable system as the cables on hydraulic brakes perform better and don't require any attention.

Setting up hydraulic disc brakes, bleeding the system and changing hoses can be messy, so make sure you do this in a suitable environment and put something on the floor to soak up spillage. Wear an apron and some silicone rubber gloves, as brake fluid is not kind to your skin.

Why bleed a disc brake?

The mushy, weak feeling at the brakes is due to air caught in the system. The disc systems on many new bikes need bleeding because there will be a lot of air in the hoses. This air will not just affect the feel at the lever, but will also absorb power. Therefore, your brakes will lose power and modulation, so bleeding is essential for peak performance.

The Shimano system uses mineral oil, not DOT4 or 5 fluid. Do not mix fluids and always use the manufacturer's recommended fluid. Don't mix bleed kits either, as DOT fluid can be corrosive and can contaminate mineral oil kits, while mineral oils do not damage your paint. DOT fluid is very bad for your skin. Performance wise, there's not a lot in it.

Tools required:
- brake fluid (follow your bike manufacturer's recommendations)
- 8 mm ring wrench
- syringe and fluid piping
- bleed kits (the ones with syringes are the simplest to use as they allow you to regulate the flow of liquid and keep an eye on how much fluid you have left to flush through. However, bleed kits aren't totally essential, and as you get more confident you will no doubt develop your own techniques. The quick-bleed method on page 85 will save you time and requires no special clamps or hoses.)

Using a bleed kit

1 Turn the brake lever so that the reservoir on the handle is level with the ground. Then remove the cover and the rubber plate (or diaphragm) underneath. This will expose the fluid and the piston camber next to the lever. Unscrew the lever-reach adjusters so that the pistons will allow enough fluid into the system.

2 Center the hole in the bleed clamp cover over the reservoir, which has a foam seal on it that clamps up to leave your hands free and prevent any fluid escaping. Hook the overflow bottle on the handlebars and you're ready to bleed. This is a Shimano bleed kit, but it can be used on other systems.

3 You need to leave the pads in place while you bleed the system so you can feel the action during the process and once you've finished. Cover the pads with a clean cloth and make sure that no fluid can contaminate the rotor or the disc pads. Contaminated pads must be replaced. Some systems come with a spacer to use instead of the rotor and pads – use this if you have one as it will ensure the pads do not get contaminated.

4 Place the hose of the full syringe over the bleed nipple on the caliper, then open the valve with a wrench. Slowly push the oil into the system, then pull the brake lever carefully two or three times to bed everything in. Continue pushing until there's about 10 cc left in the syringe, then jiggle the plunger back and forth so it's free of air. Finally, pull the plunger back slightly to suck some fluid back.

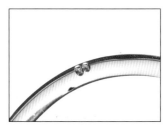

5 The excess oil will pass through the tube on the bleed clamp and into the bottle. Stop when the fluid runs clear, without any bubbles in it.

6 Now check the 'bite' of the brake – that is, where the pads hit the rotor. It should feel positive and smooth without any give at the levers. If it still feels mushy, pump the lever several times and repeat step 4 to make sure the air is out of the system. Top up the reservoir so it is full to the top edge of the unit. Be careful not to introduce any air bubbles, which may mean you have to start again.

7 Replace the rubber cover and the reservoir cap and tighten the screws. Clean any excess fluid off the handlebars, levers and grips with some disc cleaning fluid. Dispose of any used fluid properly – ask your local bike shop where they take theirs, or call the local waste authority. Do not pour brake fluid, or any non-water-soluble oils, down the drain.

Or try the quick-bleed method...

1 Follow steps on pages 83–84, then make an overflow bucket using an old plastic cup and a coat hanger. You can also just wrap a plastic bag over the handlebars (many pro-team mechanics do this), but this creates a lot of mess and there's no way of storing the waste fluid easily.

2 Fill a syringe with bubble-free fluid. Place a tube onto the caliper bleed nipple. Undo the valve nut and then simply push the fluid *slowly* and steadily through the syringe, to purge the system from the bottom to the top. One full syringe will refresh the system. Then tighten the nipple, follow steps 6 and 7 on page 84 and you're done.

DISC TIPS

Want more power? Fit bigger rotors

Use some brake adapters to space your calipers away from the center of the hub. This means that you can fit bigger rotors while still using your existing calipers. You can therefore increase braking power by up to 35 percent.

Pad care

When cleaning your bike or removing the wheels for transport, always remove the brake pads and set them away from any brake fluid, lube or grease. Then insert a spacer into the caliper to prevent the pistons from popping out should the lever be activated by accident. Leave the pads brake-faces together to make it even more difficult to contaminate the surfaces.

Mushy brakes – a quick-fix tip

If you don't have a bleed kit or you are short of fluid, try this quick fix. Flatten the reservoir and open the cap. Fix the brake in the full-on position with a zip tie and leave for 20–30 minutes. All the bubbles will slowly rise from inside the system. When this has finished, top up the reservoir with extra bubble-free fluid and replace the cover. The result will be sharp lever action and no mushy feel, without having to re-bleed.

Removing and replacing hoses

All hydraulic hoses follow the same replacement principles. Like bleeding, it's pretty simple to do. However, there are a few different types depending on which system you are using. Goodridge hoses are the best available for all systems. They use braided cables, which are more expensive than normal cables but give you better braking performance and a less spongy feel at the lever. They are also easier to trim and fit.

Some cable systems have factory-fitted collars, which cannot be cut. You will therefore have to specify the length of cable you need for your bike. With these systems, unlike cable-activated brakes, the amount of cable is less important to the feel at the lever. However, really long plastic cable runs do tend to flex slightly under heavy braking.

Each hose kit (enough for one brake) consists of two banjos, fixing bolts, collars, a length of hose and some O-rings. Check the manufacturer's instructions for recommended tightening torques and correct cable types before you start. Also, read through the section on bleeding (pages 83–85) as you will need to do this after the cable has been installed. Remove any brake pads and make sure that the pistons inside the calipers are flush with the inside of the caliper body. Insert a spacer into the cavity to prevent the pistons from moving.

Be careful when you remove the old cable not to splash brake fluid and, although there won't be much fluid in the system, make sure you catch any waste. Wear some gloves and safety goggles as the fluid can damage your skin.

Lastly, always check the cable for leaks before you ride. Tighten all the fittings and squeeze the levers hard. Leave the bike overnight and check for leaks the following day.

Tools required:
- **8 mm wrench**
- **sharp knife**
- **sharp cable cutters (shearing type)**
- **hacksaw (sharp)**
- **awl**
- **bleeding kit**
- **a sponge and some paper towels**
- **goggles and gloves**

1 Cut braided hoses with a set of sharp cable shears. You can also use a hacksaw with a sharp blade. Measure the new cable against the old one, or cut the cable after you have installed one end securely. Always double-check the length before you cut.

2 Cut back the plastic covering 11 mm down the hose. This will allow the outer collar to fit snugly over the braided part of the cable.

3 With a clean awl or 'poker', make sure that the internal PTFE (Teflon) liner is open enough to allow you to start inserting the spigot part at the end of the banjo.

4 The exposed braid will now fit into the collar. Be careful as you start to feed the cable into the collar not to fray the braid or trap it over the edge of the collar.

5 Push the collar down the cable, leaving a little gap so that the collar can rotate freely and thread easily onto the banjo spigot. The spigot has a tapered end to make insertion to the PTFE liner easier.

6 As the banjo reaches the threaded part of the collar, start to turn the collar to thread it onto the banjo. As the banjo travels farther down the cable you will need more force to turn it. If you have to use pliers, cover them with duct tape or electrical tape to prevent them damaging the banjo.

7 Continue to thread the banjo into the cable, retightening the collar as necessary until it has butted up to the end of the plastic cover. When the banjo has butted up to the end of the collar, lock off the collar against it.

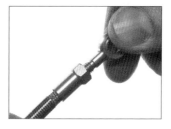

8 There are two O-rings per banjo that seal the system. The fixing bolt has a hole drilled down the center and through the middle, which allows fluid to pass into the cable from either the caliper or the lever reservoir. The cable needs to be attached carefully to the caliper or brake lever and make sure no dirt or debris gets trapped into the system.

9 On XTR levers there are two prongs that locate on either side of the banjo collar. You may have to adjust the collar slightly so that the banjo can sit flat and square through these prongs and onto the lever.

10 Set the angle of the cable before you fix the other end at the lever. Make sure that there is as smooth a line as possible, to ensure that the cable doesn't kink at the collar.

11 When fitting the banjo assembly with a straight-fitting lever, fit the non-banjo type fitting first. This makes it easier to align the banjo at the caliper to the correct angle with the final turn of the wrench.

12 Lastly, once the angles have been set on the banjos and the cables are the right length, tighten up the collars and the banjo fixing bolts. You can then bleed the system to recharge it with brake fluid.

TIPS

Magura brakes

With Magura brakes you need to push a barbed tubing insert into the open end of the cable. This can be tapped in with a plastic mallet. Use Magura brake blood for Magura hydraulic systems.

Hope cables

Hope cables use a brass olive fitting over the cable outer and a spigot that is pushed into place. This olive is locked onto the lever with a sleeve. All the same rules apply, but be careful when replacing the spigot as it is very fragile and can easily snap off. Hope systems also use DOT 5.1 hydraulic brake fluid.

7

Handlebars, grips, bar ends and seatposts

Handlebars

It is best to buy handlebars at the length you are going to use them, but some bikes come with a very wide set that you may want to cut down a little. The wider the bar, the more control you will have over the steering, but with very wide bars you may find you get stuck (literally) in the tighter sections of single tracks. Cross-country racers may also prefer a narrower bar for comfort on longer distances.

It is not recommended that you cut down carbon bars, so buy the correct length. Always measure them up to a set you are used to.

CONTACT POINTS

Tools required:
· hairspray
· an old spoke
· utility knife
· pair of scissors
· zip ties
· Griptite or touch-up paint (for permanent fixing)
· set of Allen keys

1 Handlebars should be positioned carefully, and aim to keep them as scratch-free as possible. Take care when installing them not to twist them In the stem too much as this can scratch the surface of the bar, which creates a stress riser and can fail at a later date. There is usually a mark or series of marks on the bar where the center section is. This will also give you an idea of the preferred angle of the sweep. Line this up with the front cap of the stem.

2 Center the bars in the stem. The controls can then be positioned at equal distances from the stem. Measure the position of the gear and brake shifters and set them to the correct torque fitting. Do not overtighten them, as the levers are sensitive and could bend if they are not allowed to 'move' a little in the event of a crash.

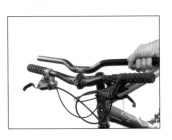

3 The main advantage of riser bars over flat bars is that they place the rider higher at the front of the bike, thus giving them a more 'controlled' position. Risers should be positioned so that the sweep faces toward the rider. Some downhill racers prefer higher and wider riser bars, as they give added control.

TIPS

- Creaking bars? Most noises from handlebars can easily be eliminated by stripping the bar from the stem, cleaning it with parts cleaner (disc-brake cleaner is good for this) and rebuilding the stem with fresh grease or copper slip on the fixing bolts. Take the stem off, check the steerer for corrosion and clean it too.
- Replace bars after bad crashes and after a couple of years of heavy use. Failure is rare, but you will not get a great deal of warning before they go – so treat them with respect. Change your bars on a regular basis as they are more likely to fail after prolonged usage.

Grips and bar ends

1 Removing your old grips is really easy. If you don't need them again, just cut them off with a utility knife. Alternatively, use an old spoke to pull the grip away from the bar then squirt some spray lube up the inside (this may need working around a bit if the grip is really stuck). Wrap some tape around the threaded bit of the spoke to stop it scratching the bars. If you are going to reuse the grip, don't use spray lube as it will only make them spin when you refit them. Use some hairspray instead.

2 If you are fitting a grip shifter or a bar end, you'll need to cut down the grip a bit. Measure it carefully next to the old grip or against the bar. Cut away the extra part carefully with a utility knife. You can tidy up the ragged end with a pair of scissors. If you are using Gripshift, place the uncut end next to the shifter. This will give you a flush fitting for better shifting.

3 Use some hairspray to fit the grips. This will allow you to push the grip on very easily, and it also sets like a lacquer and seals the grip to the bar. It's not sticky though, so it won't make a mess of your bars and so on. Some riders use car spraypaint as it seals out the water and prevents your grips from spinning, but it can be a bit messy. If you use Gripshift shifters, always use the plastic washer they provide to enable the shifter to rotate without binding to the grip.

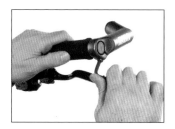

4 If you are fitting bar ends, make sure you don't overtighten them; they only need to be tight enough so you don't move them with riding force. It's best to let them move a bit to protect your bike in the event of a crash – if they are too tight then you risk twisting the bar as well as damaging the bar end. Always put a plug in the end of the bar – crashing with open-ended bars is very dangerous even if they have bar ends on them, and plugs will also stop water and mud getting into your bars.

5 Bar-end stops prevent the grip from pulling off under pressure. Locking grips are even better as they do not rotate at all. Also fit bash ends if you're into jumping or crash a lot, as they will absorb the shock and prevent the ends of the bar being damaged. A good tip is to zip-tie the grip tightly to the bar. Most grips have a slot cut into them for the bar to bed into. Use a small tie for the best results and place the knuckle bit underneath so you don't catch your hands on it. Fine-gauge wire can work just as well, but make sure you tuck it away so you don't catch your gloves or hands on the ends. Wrap the wire around the grip a couple of times before twisting the two ends tightly together.

TIPS

- When fitting bar ends, make sure you get them at a comfortable riding angle. This will usually be between 5 and 15 degrees. The best way to do this is to line them up with the angle of your stem. Try to get a position that's comfortable for cruising and climbing and bear in mind that the bar end is supposed to prevent you from bending your wrists too much. If you position them too flat, cruising becomes stretched out and uncomfortable, but if you position them too upright then climbing gets a bit cramped.
- If you want to fit bar ends to an ended type grip, the end of the grip has to be cut out so you can slide the grip along a bit. A neat way of doing this is to slide the grip onto an old bar (don't use your new one as you'll damage it) and tap the end of the grip firmly with a hammer. This will cut out the required round plug of rubber without having to use a knife. Remove the plug and push the grip onto the new bar.

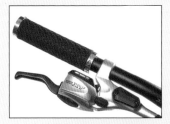

Seatposts

Materials

Seatposts are usually made out of aluminum. The best posts are made from butted Easton EA 70 tubing, 7075-T6 or 6061 T6. Cro-mo steel posts are strong and therefore great for dirt jumpers, but they do weigh a bit more. Steel is also better if you want to use an extra-long post (more than 300 mm). Some posts have carbon-fiber shafts.

Failures

The worst-case scenario is a snap, but this will usually be the result of riding around on a bent post for a while and thus placing too much stress on the material; the constant bending results in a fatigue fracture. You can easily check for a bend by placing a straight edge (e.g. a ruler) next to it and eying it up front and back and side to side.

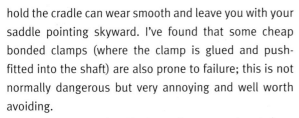

Do this regularly, especially after a crash.

The clamp can break in various places, the yokes (the two halves that clamp the saddle rails together) can snap or the serrations that hold the cradle can wear smooth and leave you with your saddle pointing skyward. I've found that some cheap bonded clamps (where the clamp is glued and push-fitted into the shaft) are also prone to failure; this is not normally dangerous but very annoying and well worth avoiding.

The seat post should always be smeared with anti-seize grease before inserting it into the seat tube. It should slide in without any pressure being applied and there shouldn't be any side-to-side movement before the clamp bolt is tightened. The anti-seize grease will also prevent the different materials from seizing together. The seatposts also need to be quickly adjustable for height – if you're riding extreme downhills or drop-offs you'll want to tuck the post well out of the way – so the grease will prevent them from seizing in the frame and getting scratched.

Length

Seatposts come in several lengths, with 300 mm, 350 mm and 400 mm being the most common. You need a post that leaves plenty of material in the frame; they usually have a line to indicate the minimum insertion level (or Max. Ht.). Do not exceed this – it not only protects the seatpost, but also prevents placing excess strain on the top of the frame's seat tube/clamp area, which can easily be distorted by the extra leverage on the little bit left in the frame.

Size (diameter)

This depends on the material that the frame is made of. Steel and standard aluminum frames usually come in 26.4–27.2 mm sizes, but some specialist frames can be as little as 25 mm and as much as 32.7 mm. Getting the recommended size for your frame is essential, as even 0.2 mm either way can make a difference to the correct fit. If it is too big, it can swell the seat tube and make it difficult to fit or remove; if it is too small, it can move about and damage the collar and distort the top of the seat tube.

Pedals

Mountain bike pedals get a lot of abuse. They are invariably the first thing to hit the ground when you crash and, as they stick out from the bike at the bottom of your pedal stroke, they bash stuff like rocks and logs as you hammer through a single track.

Toe clips and straps are, thankfully, now less popular. They were dangerous if tightened up too much. Most mountain bikers now use SPD-type (Shimano Pedaling Dynamics) pedals, as they offer the most efficient power transfer – they let you pull as well as push because you are clipped into the pedal. The cleat is recessed into the sole of the shoe so you can walk or run up hills.

Flat pedals are more robust. They have their roots in BMX bikes, so they tend to be more popular with dirt jumpers and trials riders. The control and simplicity of the flat pedal means that they are better suited to this type of riding.

Most pedals have the same axle size, although old-school BMX pedals have slightly smaller threads than mountain bike versions.

Tools required:
- waterproof synthetic or anti-seize grease
- torque wrench
- Allen key
- lubricant
- pedal collar tool
- vise
- grease
- wrenches

1 Before you start, remember that pedals have a left- and right-hand thread. Most systems stamp 'L' and 'R' on the axle somewhere so you know which is which. This refers to side of the bike that the pedal is supposed to go on. On Shimano pedals the stamp is usually on the flat part of the pedal spindle, where the wrench attaches.

2 Pedal threads must be greased. Use a quality waterproof synthetic or an anti-seize grease. Clean the threads and regrease them regularly. Because axles are made out of steel and cranks are made out of aluminum, there can be problems with threads. Be careful not to cross-thread the cranks as they will be ruined.

3 Left- and right-hand pedals have different threads. The drive-side (right-hand) pedal is a right-hand thread, that is it tightens up in the direction of pedaling. The non-drive-side (left-hand) pedal is a left-hand thread, which also tightens in the direction of pedaling. The easiest way to remember this is to hold the pedal up to the crank, flat on your fingers, and spin the cranks backwards as if you were freewheeling.

4 Tighten the pedals to the manu-facturer's recom-mended torque setting. Hold the opposite crank or the rear wheel and use the added leverage to help you tighten the pedals. To remove the pedals, it is probably easiest if you stand the bike on the floor. You will remove the pedal in the direction of the freewheel, so you may have to hold the opposite crank to prevent it from spinning.

5 If you are using SPD pedals for the first time, back the springs off so that the release tension is minimal. As the pedal is double-sided and has a spring for each side, make sure you loosen the bolts on either side of the pedal.

6 Regular cleaning and lubrication is essential. Rebuild the bearings regularly, but replace the bearings every time you service the pedals to keep them rolling for longer.

7 Binding and loose bearings are usually the telltale signs of a bent axle. Most Shimano pedals use the same cartridge-style axle, which can be replaced. There is a special tool to undo the collars on the pedals. Place this in a vise for ease of use.

8 Place the special collar tool in a vise and loosen the pedal (there is an arrow on the pedal collar to show you which direction to turn it). The pedal body can be removed and cleaned thoroughly with degreaser and a toothbrush.

9 With the axle removed, you can assess the damage. Hold the bearing part and spin the axle stub. If it is wobbly and the bearings are very loose, you will probably have to replace the complete assembly.

10 Remove the lock nut and the top cone. If the bearings are dull and pitted and the cones have similar pitting and marks, you will be better off replacing the complete unit. You can adjust the cones with this special tool or with the appropriate sized wrenches. It's a very tricky job and it's very easy to lose the $3/32$-inch bearings. If you are stripping the axle, you'll need fresh bearings and grease. Readjusting the cones is very similar to adjusting wheel bearings. You are looking to set the collar so it has no play and isn't binding onto the bearings.

11 Before replacing a new axle or the restored old one, pack the pedal body with grease.

12 Finally, tighten the pedal body onto the axle using the same tool. You only need to tighten it by hand – overtightening can break the collar and bind the bearings.

TIPS

· Noisy or creaking pedals can be due to worn cleats or simply dry threads. Regrease the threads regularly and replace your cleats before they start to release on their own. It's not only annoying, it can also be dangerous.
· The cleat on the side you release most often when you stop will wear more quickly than the other one, so swap them around for a longer life.

SPD (Shimano Pedaling Dynamics)

This is another significant Shimano 'invention'. Shimano took the clipless cleat idea from the road pedals of the late eighties and made it into a system that you can walk in, as well as cycle. Now used by millions of mountain bikers, this has to be one of the most useful mountain bike inventions. Efficient pedaling and a mud-clearing design make for a very user-friendly system.

SPD pedal cleats

Once you have installed the pedals, you can fit the cleats to your shoes. Most shoes now have an open sole, but some still have a rubber cover over the cleat box. If this is the case, you will have to cut the cover away with a utility knife.

Regular cleaning and lubrication is essential. Pick out all the jammed-in mud and grit from the sole around the cleat. Lubricate the cleats regularly to prevent them from rusting up, as rust will wear the pedal and cleat out more quickly.

Tools required:
· **anti-seize grease**
· **pen**
· **torque wrench**
· **duct tape**
· **drill**
· **vise**
· **utility knife**

1 Assess the position of the ball of your foot over the pedal axle. Mark on the side of your shoe where the ball of your foot is, then mark a line across the sole of your shoe. This is where the cleat will be placed. Use this reference to decide which set of holes in the plates to use.

2 Prepare the threads in the plates with an anti-seize grease. Copper Slip is best. The cleats will rust pretty quickly if you don't. You can replace these screws with stainless steel bolts (you can buy these from an engineering supplier) as they are less likely to rust up and will therefore last longer.

3 Tighten the shoe cleats to the recommended torque setting. Do not overtighten them as the threads can strip very easily, in which case you would have to replace the sole insert.

4 Some shoes don't have a shoe-cleat plate inside the sole. To insert (or replace) this, you must work from the inside of the shoe. Lift up the part of the insole behind the cleat box and push the plate in so that it fits into the slots in the sole.

5 It's worth covering the insole with duct tape to seal the hole and prevent your foot rubbing on the back of the cleat box.

6 Drilling out old, seized-in bolts is the only way to remove cleats once the heads are rounded off. Basically, drill the bolt head until it disappears. Once the head is off, the cleat will drop off. You can then remove the threaded bit left in the shoe. Sometimes the insert in the shoe is worth replacing too.

7 The correct cleat position is with the ball or pushing part of your foot over the pedal axle. This requires measuring and some trial and error to get it right. It's also best to get someone to help you do this job, as you can only adjust the cleat position properly once the cleats are in place.

8

Tires

Size

Apart from Gary Fisher's 29-inch (twenty-niner) wheel, most mountain bike tires are 26 inches in diameter, but they come in a variety of sizes. Thick or thin, the size of your tires can help you get there first. The law for racing states that 1.5 inches is the narrowest allowed, but how do you measure them? Like most theories, no-one can decide on a trade-compatible system for measuring the width of mountain bike tires. Tire size is not normally the width across the treads, as you would think, but is based more on the size of the casings. Some have higher profiles and others more rubber on the tread, which makes them appear larger.

WHEELS AND TIRES

There are industry standards, but everybody seems to ignore them and uses their own methods for measuring instead. Unfortunately, this leaves the customer a bit confused to say the least, and means manufacturers can size their tires according to current trends. The key is to find the size that suits the riding you're doing and try to see the tire blown up on a wheel before you buy.

The European Tyre and Rim Technical Organisation (ETRTO) and the International Standards Organisation (ISO) use the same method to determine tire width: take the distance between the two beads, measured over the tire tread, and divide it by 2.5. However, some manufacturers take the measurement on the casing side from the edge of the bead to the center of the casing, thus some of their tires can look larger as they use the same casing volume but larger treads.

Beading

All tires have a bead that runs around the edge of the tire and secures the tire by locking under the lip of the rim. Steel beads keep a circular shape and Kevlar beads are flexible, but both have similar strength. Steel-beaded tires are slightly flexible so they stretch onto the rim; Kevlar doesn't stretch so the beads are made a bit longer, which helps but can make the procedure a bit of a handful. The main advantage with Kevlar is the weight you can save, and you can carry folded spares for longer trips. The main disadvantage is the price – Kevlar is an advanced material and costs much more.

Mavic's tubeless system will eventually become more widespread. It does take a little more preparation time than a standard wheel, but the result is a far better system and less chance of pinch flats and other inner tube problems. See pages 103–6 for more on UST tires.

Compounds

Different colored tires often denote different hardness of the rubber compound. Some riders find softer rubber means much better grip on hardpacked surfaces. Black tires are harder than these and tend to last longer, but the quality of rubber can have a big effect on the amount of grip and wear rate of your tires. This is often reflected in the price.

Softer and lighter racing tires are more susceptible to flats and tend to wear more quickly. There's always a trade-off when trying to improve grip and lighten weight. Assess the variables and choose a tread for its ride quality and value rather than its 'pose' appeal.

Tread

When mountain bikes first started out, the only tread patterns available were fairly limited – studded balloon tires were about it. Nowadays there are hundreds of combinations available, which cover just about all eventualities from deserts to snowstorms. The norm these days seems to be an arrow-style front and a scoop-type rear. Some are dual purpose, so you can change the back for the front as they start to wear out.

Everybody has their personal favorite, so try out as many as you can and use a tread pattern that suits your type of riding.

Fat or thin

Tread patterns are also affected by the section of the tire; a tire's width and height can alter your bike's handling characteristics just as much as the tread itself. Fatter tires give a bit more suspension to the ride, but also provide a larger surface area for drag, punctures and mud clogging, while thinner tires will go faster but transfer more shock through to your hands. Heavier riders may prefer the fatter option, but lighter people won't need so much cushioning.

Pressure

Tire pressure for mountain bikes is often overlooked, but it can have a major effect on the handling and stability of your bike. Too much air gives you a fast ride but only at the expense of comfort, and leaves you vulnerable to impact punctures, while too little air gives a squashy, sluggish but comfortable ride that may pick up thorns and can snakebite puncture more easily.

You can afford to use higher pressures with suspension bikes as the travel will eat up the shock, but if you ride with rigid forks you will need to take more care. Look at the recommended pressures on the sidewall of the tire and stick within the limits. Experiment with different conditions and pressures – try harder, narrower tires for fast conditions and mud and softer, wider tires for technical conditions or when you need more grip.

Directional

There are two types of directional tires, front- or rear-specific or dual purpose (the same tread for front and rear use). Usually, directional tires have a rotation arrow on the sidewall. If no arrows are apparent then the rule of thumb is to fit them with the arrow patterns pointing forwards in the direction of rotation.

UST Tires

UST (Universal Standard Tubeless) is now an industry standard for mountain bike tires. It is designed to eliminate the need for an inner tube. This has obvious advantages and, when installed correctly, is pretty foolproof. Some expect that this type of technology will be standard on most mountain bikes before too long.

The tires will have a recommended pressure range, for example 30–70 PSI. It is possible to run UST tires at lower pressures than usual tires because they are less likely to get snakebite punctures as you hit the rim on rocks and roots. However, do not run the tire at lower than the recommended pressure as the air can escape. Equally, don't run the tires over the maximum pressure, as this will place extra pressure on the seals and the valve.

Be aware that UST tires can deflate over time and you will have to check the tire pressure before every ride. I think this is a good idea if you are using standard tubes too, as running tires at their recommended pressures prevents punctures and will make sure your bike handles predictably. Changing your tires regularly is expensive, but it is the best way to ensure decent performance from UST systems.

Tubeless tires

This is one of the most significant developments of the past few years. The tire is sealed to the rim and the spoke holes are configured in a double-walled rim, so that an airtight seal is possible. This means you can do away with the weak link – the inner tube. Tubeless tires are very popular with racers as they only fail if the tire gashes very badly. This technology will get better and better and eventually make punctures a rare event.

Tools required:
· a bucket of soapy water to help seal the tire to the rim (do not use a strong detergent as it will damage the anodizing on the rim; use a simple soap instead, or shampoo works quite well!)
· Vaseline to wet the valve
· a decent floor pump
· spoke wrench
Note: Never use tire levers on UST tires as they can damage the bead and the seal of the tire to the rim.

Putting UST tires on

1 Because the UST double-walled rim is sealed and there is no access to the spoke nipples through the inside of the rim, the nipples are oversized and thread directly into the rim. This means you will have to true the wheel with this special spoke wrench, but also means that you can replace a spoke without having to remove the tires.

2 The UST tire is a little heavier than a standard tire and has a more substantial side wall and a fatter bead than a standard tire. As with a standard tire you will need to check the direction arrows on the side wall. You must only use ISO-compatible tires, but most of the main manufacturers have a UST option in their product lines.

3 The valve is the key element to the tubeless wheel, and Mavic recommends you replace this valve at least once a year. It has to be a 6.5 mm diameter valve with a Presta head.

4 The rubber flange of the valve has to sit inside the gorge in the middle of the rim. A little soapy water or Vaseline on the rubber seal will help seal the valve and the rim. Here you can see the gorge that runs around the base of the rim – this helps to install the tire bead. Also notice the absence of spoke holes.

5 There is an 'O' ring that fits over the valve to seal it to the rim. Check that this is in place over the join between the rim and the valve, and replace it on a regular basis. Moisten it slightly with some Vaseline to help it seal the air in completely.

6 The lock ring is tightened on top of the 'O' ring. This should only be done up finger tight. It is possible to fit a Schraeder valve adaptor to the Presta-size valve, but the UST system can only be used with the UST valve.

7 Soap the rim with some very diluted soapy water. Then, starting opposite the valve hole, place one side of the tire bead over the rim and into the gorge in the middle of the rim. If you push the bead into this gorge, it makes it far easier to pull the tire onto the rim as it adds some slack to the bead. Work with both hands around the rim towards the valve hole. Do not be tempted to use tire levers; the tire should go on with minimal force.

8 Once one side of the tire is on, push the bead away from the gorge so that the other bead can use it. Run your finger around the gorge inside the rim and push the bead firmly towards the other side of the rim. Then, starting opposite the valve hole again, insert the remaining bead, forcing it into the gorge again so that once you reach the valve hole there will be enough slack to pull the tire on easily.

9 Pulling the final bit on is tricky, so be careful not to damage the tire bead at this point. You may have to force the tire on a little, but if the bead has been placed into the gorge correctly it should be pretty easy. Sometimes it pays to remove the tire and start again. If the tire is too tight, work both sides of the wheel around to the valve hole until there is a small amount left to pull on. You may need to add a little more soapy water to assist this bit.

10 Seat the tire into the rim and check that it is evenly tucked into the beads of the rim on either side of the wheel. Put a couple of puffs of air into the tire and spin the wheel to check it is running true. If there are any lumps in the tire, you may have to let the air out again and re-seat it.

11 Pull the tire around the rim slightly, pushing it from side to side a little. Do this quite vigorously as it will show you whether the tire has seated nicely into the rim. Pay particular attention to the valve area, as the end of the valve can push the tire out of the rim when you start to inflate.

12 New tires will seal very quickly as you start pumping. Check that the sidewall is positioned equally around the rim (there is usually a line molded into the sidewall of the tire to use as a guide). Undo the valve completely and pump the tire up. Inflate the tire quickly, using a floor pump if you can. The tire may 'pop' a few times as it reaches a decent pressure, but don't worry as it will find its shape as it reaches maximum inflation.

Removing a UST tire

Deflate the tire and, starting opposite the valve hole, unlock one side of the tire bead by forcing it into the gorge in the middle of the rim. Work it around the rim and then unhook it by the valve. Then unlock the second bead by pushing it into the gorge and working it around the wheel. This is usually a very easy process.

Using a standard tube with a UST tire

1. Repairing the UST tire involves patching the inside of the tire as you would a regular tube. There are several products especially made for this, including pre-glued patches, which will get you home if you puncture on the trail.

2. It is possible to use a standard tube as a spare, in case the tire is damaged (ripped) beyond repair. It's pretty rare for this to happen, but on long trail rides you should carry a spare tube just in case.

3. Remember that you must not use tire levers if you want to be able to reuse the tire.

4. Only use a Presta valve tube as the hole in the rim will only take this type of valve. Drilling out the hole to take a Schraeder valve will ruin the rim and it will not seal properly.

Troubleshooter

If the tire is leaking rapidly, check the following:

- Gashes in the sidewall, even if they don't go through the tire completely, can leak slowly and will reduce the performance of the tire. Have a good look around the whole tire and patch any that may seem suspect.
- Check the bead seating. Inflate the tire to 10 per cent more than the maximum recommended pressure. Then deflate the tire completely. The bead should remain firmly tucked into the rim edge and retain the seal. If it doesn't, the bead may be damaged.
- Clean the rim and bead with soapy water and replace the tire as recommended.
- Check the rims for dents or scratches.
- Lastly, if these tips don't help, inflate the tire to about 50 PSI and submerge it in the bath. Any holes will show up pretty quickly.

Replacing spokes

Replacing a spoke is a straightforward operation, but it can be time consuming. Spokes will give little warning before they snap, and the usual causes are previous damage or uneven spoke tension due to rim damage or repeated heavy impacts.

As broken spokes usually happen as a wheel is reaching the end of its serviceable life, it's worth considering a rebuild after you break one. Repeated spoke failure (where you have broken several spokes one after the other) usually means that the rim is wrecked and the spokes are struggling to support it. Properly built wheels from a good wheel builder will not break spokes, unless the spokes are damaged somehow. Properly tensioned hand-built wheels are less likely to fail and they are a wise investment.

Broken spokes usually occur on the drive side of the rear wheel. With singlespeed wheels and 150 mm rear axles, broken spokes are becoming less common as there is less dish in the rear wheel and therefore the spokes are under less strain on the drive side.

Tools required:
· **spoke wrench**
· **spare spokes (make sure you have the correct length)**
· **screwdriver and/or nipple driver**
· **truing stand**

1 In emergencies, you can replace the spoke with the tire in place, but only if you have exactly the right length of spoke. It's always best to remove the tire, tube and rim tape so that you can access the nipple and replace it if necessary. Over-long spokes will protrude into the rim cavity and burst the tube so make sure you take care when picking the replacement spoke.

2 If the spoke is outbound (the head of the spoke faces into the hub center) you will have to thread the spoke in from the opposite side of the wheel. This is the easiest way to lace the spoke into the wheel.

3 The spoke can pass through the lower part of the spokes on the opposite side of the wheel. The spoke will then usually travel over the first two crossing spokes and under the last one before reaching the rim.

4 Inbound spokes (where the head of the spoke faces out from the hub center) are far more tricky to lace. You have to angle the spoke upward so that it avoids the crossing at the other side of the wheel. Be careful not to bend the spoke too much as this will weaken it.

5 Spokes cross three times between the hub and the rim. Depending on the way the wheel has been laced, the spokes will cross under twice and over once or over twice and under once. Either way, it is essential that you copy this lacing when you replace a spoke to maintain the integrity and strength of the wheel.

6 In order to lace the spoke around the rim, you will have to push it under the rim. Protect the rim from being scratched by the threads when you do this by placing a finger or thumb over the end of the spoke, at the same time bending the spoke very gently and evenly so that it can tuck under the rim.

7 In this photograph the replacement spoke is positioned behind the final crossing spoke and is long enough to insert into the rim cavity through the eyelet.

8 The correct length spoke will meet the rim eyelet and should be long enough to pass through the nipple and be level with the top of it on the inside of the rim. Any longer and the spoke will be too slack on the nipple. The nipple can be replaced if necessary; nipples can round off with poorly fitting spoke wrenches and poor quality nipples can shear off.

9 Take up the slack with a screwdriver before you start to true the wheel. Make a note of how far the other spokes protrude from the nipple and – if you have the correct length spoke – you can get the spoke to a similar position. See pages 108–11 for more on truing wheels.

10 Eyeletted rims last longer than non-eyeletted ones and experience fewer breakages as the eyelets allow the nipples to move slightly inside the rim. The eyelets also reinforce the rim and are easier to true as the nipples move freely inside them.

TIPS

- Always have another wheel handy so you can copy the spoke pattern, especially if you are replacing more than one spoke.
- Use a nipple driver to run nipples onto the spoke threads. Stop when the nipple just reaches the end of the threaded section.
- Carefully bed in the elbows of the spokes by using either your thumb or the face of a plastic mallet.
- Use brass washers (DT make these) on loose spoke holes. Some wheel builders 'set' the nipples into the holes with a nail punch – be careful though when using bonded or lightweight hubs.
- Adjust your rear derailleur if the chain over-shifts from the lowest gears and into the spokes. This can damage the spokes, and cause them to break at a later date. Also, if the rear derailleur hits the spokes it can rip the gear mechanism off and/or ruin the wheel, so adjust it even if it makes the slightest noise.

Truing wheels

Much as I love wheel building, this is not the place to show you how to do it. Gerd Schraener's *The Art of Wheelbuilding* and Jobst Brandt's *The Bicycle Wheel* both offer excellent instruction and guidance in this very technical process. Wheel building is involved rather than difficult; some would say it is much more of an art than a science, but the fact that there are complete books written on the subject speaks for itself. So, here I will show you the basics of wheel truing and hope you'll get the bug and want to learn more about how wheels are built.

First, assess the wheel and decide where the imbalance could be. Spin the wheel and see where the buckles are and where the wheel has uneven tension. A wheel is like a suspension bridge and any imbalance in the supports (spokes) places more stress on the neighboring supports. The most common problem is a broken spoke, but spokes can also be loose or damaged, which will also cause a wobble.

When you spin the wheel, it should sit centrally in the jig (or bike if you are on the trail), so your job is to find out where, and more importantly how, the wheel is being pulled away from this center line. Do not attempt to true a wheel until you have a good idea what is causing the buckle. **Lateral** (side to side) buckles are the easiest to solve:

· if the wheel hops to the left, tighten the spoke on the right or loosen the spoke on the left;
· if the wheel hops to the right, tighten the spoke on the left or loosen the spoke on the right.

However, **radial** (up and down) buckles are a little different:
· if the hop is *toward* the hub, the spoke is too tight;
· if the hop is *away* from the hub, the spoke is too loose.

So, if the rim hops to the left and towards the hub at the same time, there is a spoke pulling too tightly on the left, and if the rim hops to the right and away from the hub at the same time, there is a loose spoke on the right.

That is the simple version; the rest is about practice and experience – just like tuning a piano, apparently. The first few times you true a wheel will take you some time, but if you can be patient (and practice) it will become second nature. Remember to make small adjustments at first and mark the rim with chalk or wrap a strip of tape on the suspect spokes so that you always know where you started.

Rear wheels have tighter spokes on the drive side than they do on the non-drive side. The non-drive spokes are also longer. This means that they require fewer turns than the drive side; it depends on the wheel but the ratio is about 2:1. On front hubs you will always need to loosen or tighten the same amount on both sides. Whatever you do, do it gradually and in no more than quarter- or half-turns at a time.

Tools required:
· **truing stand**
· **spoke wrenches (there are a variety of nipple sizes depending on spoke type and gauge)**
· **dishing stick**
· **spoke tension meter (optional)**

1 Treat the spokes in groups rather than individually. The usual cause of a buckle is a broken spoke (for more on replacing spokes see pages 107–8); however, here we are trying to find the loose ones that may just require tightening. Grab several spokes at a time and squeeze them to feel where the problem is before you start to true the wheel.

2 Always use a spoke wrench that fits the nipples snugly. A loose-fitting key will ruin the nipple very easily, especially if the nipple is tight. If the spoke becomes very tight and the rim still needs to move some more, you may have to loosen the opposite spoke to allow a little more movement. Spokes tighten with a standard right-hand thread, so if you are using your right hand you will need to turn the spoke wrench toward you to tighten the spoke and away from you to loosen it.

3 A severe radial hop or a skip in the rim can signify a set or group of very loose or tight spokes. As with the lateral truing, you need careful judgment to decide which spokes to tackle first. Grab hold of a few and try to find the loose ones first. Then, using quarter-turns only, adjust the tension in two or four spokes at a time – you need to pull on both sides equally to prevent the wheel going out laterally as well as radially.

4 'Dish' describes the shape of the wheel. Basically, the hub lock nuts (where the wheel is held in the frame or forks) and the rim need to sit in line for the bike to handle properly. Wheel dish is determined by measuring the wheel with a dishing stick, which checks that the lock nuts are equally spaced on either side of the rim. Dish guarantees that the wheels will run in line and also allows for efficient braking. Disc brakes take up space on the non-drive side of the wheel, but this can reduce the dish and therefore create more equal tension in the wheel, which is a good thing.

5 Rim dents and wear to the braking surfaces will make a difference to the tension in the wheel. Dents usually happen when the wheel pinch punctures due to hitting a root or a rock. Mountain bike wheels will absorb a lot of shock and the rims are made from very strong heat-treated alloys, so the chances are the rim will dent rather than collapse.

6 Accurate truing has to be done using a quality wheel jig rather than with the wheel still in the bike. Wheel jigs provide more stability, so the wheel doesn't rock around when you spin it. The wheel jig pictured here has self-centering jaws and retaining arms so that the rim will be perfect if it is trued to the guides. The jaws can be adjusted so that the rim drags on them to give you a visual and audible clue as to where the buckle is.

7 Professional wheel builders will use a DT spoke tension meter. This can accurately measure spoke tension and enables a good wheel builder to keep variation in spoke tension to around 10 per cent. This is also useful when truing a wheel, as you can assess which spokes are being pushed too hard and are therefore likely to break first.

8 Once you are happy that the wheel is round again, 'stress' the wheel in your lap or gently on the floor. Do not stress the wheel with your full weight, especially if the bearings are sealed as they are vulnerable to side loads. You will hear the wheel click and ping as the spokes 'find' their position. This may mean that the rim moves a little, so double-check it in the jig before you're finished.

9 Finally, replace the rim tape. I always use tape that will stick to the rim; this way you know it will not come loose and move around under the tube. Plastic tape is better than cloth as cloth tape holds water and will rust the eyelets, which in turn can seize the nipples. Rim tape should be renewed every time it is removed – never reuse old tape.

Rim health

Most rims designed for use with rim brakes have a wear indicator, which is either a black line or a series of dots on the middle of the rim. As the rim wears, these marks very slowly disappear, and when you can't see them anymore then the rim needs changing. It is very important to keep an eye on this, as the rims can wear severely and, combined with the pressure in the tire, the bead on the rim will eventually fail. This can be catastrophic. The tube immediately explodes and the tire is blown off the rim. The remaining part of the rim can easily tangle in the frame and, if it's the front wheel, you can have a very nasty accident. For this reason I'd say that disc brakes are far more reliable and will provide longer lasting wheels than rim-braked ones. Don't risk setting off with old rims and wheels – strong wheels will save you a long walk home.

Front hubs

Front hub cones and bearing hubs are very simple to service. The first few times can be challenging, but experience really speeds the process up. The key is to make sure that all the components are in top condition – any wear and tear to the cones or bearings means that the parts should be replaced.

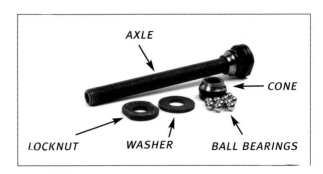

AXLE

CONE

LOCKNUT   WASHER   BALL BEARINGS

How often should I strip the hubs?

Hubs will need a complete service every 4–6 months depending on weather conditions and how often you ride. Fresh grease and regular adjustment will keep hubs rolling for a long time. Shimano cone hubs are excellent because you can rebuild them very easily and quickly and they use top quality bearings and hardened steel cones. Look after them properly and they'll easily outlast the spokes and the rims.

Loose hubs do not last very long. Grab your wheel by the tire and shake the wheel from side to side while it is still in the bike. If you feel a slight knock or 'play' through the tire, the hub is loose. This means that the bearings are bashing around inside the hub and slowly disintegrating, and the seals are more exposed, allowing water and muck into the hub. Leave the hub like this and it won't take long for the internals to fail completely. Rebuilding the wheel with a new hub is far more costly and time-consuming than replacing the grease and the bearings every few months.

Tools required:
- **2 x 13 mm cone wrenches (Shimano uses 13 mm cones, but they can vary in size)**
- **torque wrench**
- **17 mm open-ended wrench (or cone wrench)**
- **grease**
- **axle vise and bench mounted vise**

1 The key to easy hub servicing is only working on one side. If you keep one side intact, the spacing over the lock nuts is easier to retain. A front hub measures 100 mm over the lock nuts; this measurement is critical so that the wheel can easily be replaced in the forks.

2 Cone wrenches are very thin and flat. This means that they can fit into the machined flats on the sides of the cone and can adjust and tighten the cones without snagging on the washer and lock nut. Use the correct size and don't use cone wrenches to remove your pedals, as this will damage them. Hold the cone with a cone wrench and release the lock nut with a 17 mm wrench.

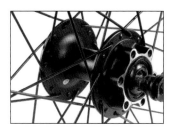

3 Undo and remove the lock nut, then the washer and, finally, the cone. The cone is made from hardened steel and has a highly polished bearing surface. Inspect the cone carefully for any rough patches on the surface, which is known as pitting. On most front wheels there is only a cone, washer and lock nut.

4 Remove the cone, spacers and – very carefully – the axle. I find it's best to do this over something that will catch the bearings should they fall out. Place the threaded components down on the workbench or over an Allen key in the order they came off the hub to help you remember the order to return them. Clean the axle and cones, leaving one side on the axle and in one piece. Keep all the bearings so that you can check you are replacing the same size and quantity.

5 Clean the inside of the bearing surfaces and inspect for damage. If the bearing surfaces and cones are pitted, you will need to replace either the cones or the hub assembly. Replacing the cones and the bearings and resetting them in grease will usually solve any hub roughness.

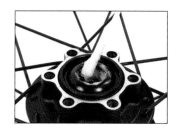

6 You do not have to remove the hub seals – they are factory fitted and are very hard to replace properly as they are pressed into the shell of the hub, and it is possible to see into the hub with the seals in place. However, if you do have to remove them, be very careful. Wrap a rag around a tire lever and pry the seals out carefully. Don't use a screwdriver as they can bend the seal, and if that happens you'll never get it back in again. To replace the seal, use your fingers to locate it and then tap it home using a rubber mallet.

7 It is good practice to replace the bearings after every strip down. The bearings are slightly more vulnerable than the cones and the hub surfaces, so they tend to wear out first. Look at them closely and you will see tiny potholes. Bearings need to be mirror finished, so if they are even slightly dull they need replacing. It's useful to have a magnetic screwdriver for this job, as they make reinstallation far easier. Store spare bearings on a magnet to make them easier to manage.

8 When all the bearings are installed, take the loose cone and push it back into the hub. Rotate it a couple of times to seat the bearings. This will also tell you if there is any damage to the bearing surface inside the hub, and will stick the bearings in place so you can turn the wheel over to do the other side. Next, double-check that there are the right amount of bearings in the hub. Lastly, smear a little more grease on top of the bearings and check there isn't any grease inside the hub. You will then be able to push the axle through without making a big mess.

9 Replace the axle (remember to return it in the same way it was removed). As you have only disturbed one set of bearings, the spacing will not have been altered. Screw the cone onto the axle and up to the bearings. Spin the axle in your fingers and 'rock' it slightly from side to side – you are looking for the point at which there is no 'play', only smooth spinning. When you are happy that the bearings are running smoothly, replace the washer and then the lock nut. At this stage they need to be finger tight.

10 With practice, you will be able to set the cones like this and simply do up the cone as in step 2. However, when you tighten the lock nut for the last time, you may also either loosen the cone slightly or tighten it. Mountain bike hubs have seals in the hub body that will drag a little when the cone is set. To set the cones properly you will need two cone wrenches (13 mm for front hubs); with two wrenches you can work the cones against each other. So, if you overtighten the lock nut, place the two cone wrenches on either side of the hub and slightly undo the cones until the axle spins freely.

TIPS

Hubs
Replace the wheel into the bike and check for play by rocking the wheel from side to side. Then pick up the bike and spin the wheel quickly. Hold onto either fork leg. You may feel a rumbling of vibration through the fork, in which case the cones are too tight. Recheck the cones again after your first ride.

Using an axle vise to hold the wheel steady will help if your hub isn't built into a wheel but isn't necessary if the wheel is complete. Axle vices are made from a soft material and clamp the axle tightly so you can work on the hub with both hands, which will speed things up. The best way to work on a hub as a part of the wheel is on top of a workbench with the hub at a slight angle so you can see into the internals.

Grease
Every mechanic has a favorite hub grease. The secret is to use a specially formulated synthetic bicycle grease that is waterproof and of a consistent quality but also not to overdo it as this can make the bearings drag and adjustment more difficult. Many of the non-synthetic or engineering-type greases are too heavy for hub bearings. Also, avoid lithium (usually white-colored) grease, as it is easily washed out of the bearings and breaks down after repeated revolutions. Shimano hub grease is excellent as is Finish Line, Park, Pedros and Rock 'n' Roll. Use a grease gun with a fine nozzle to direct grease where you want it; this will avoid waste.

Rear hubs

Much of the information in the front hub section (see pages 112–14) applies to rear hubs too. The process is the same, even though the unit is bigger. Shimano freewheel cassette bodies can be replaced, which can prolong their life indefinitely.

Rear hub spacing is usually 135 mm across the lock nuts. However, some full suspension bikes are now using 150 mm spacing as this can accommodate the disc brakes and cassette and manages to reduce the dish in the rear wheel considerably. This makes for a much stronger wheel. Shimano hubs are still all 135 mm, although some Saint and Done group sets use bolt-through axles and have 150 mm options.

If both cones need to be replaced, it is worth measuring the position of the lock nut and cones before you start work. Measure the distance from the end of the axle to the side of the first lock nut. Then, when you start to remove the cones, work on one side at a time and place the components down in the order that they are removed. I thread them over a screwdriver or an Allen key in reverse order, which makes replacement easy.

Tools required:

- cone wrenches (the Shimano rear hub has 15 mm cones, but they do vary in size)
- 17 mm open-ended wrench (or cone wrench)
- 10 mm Allen key
- grease
- axle vise and bench-mounted vise
- cassette service and replacement tools
- chain whip
- cassette lock ring tool and wrench
- torque wrench

Cones are a specific size and you must use the correct part, otherwise the hub will not work properly. So, if you have to replace anything, check that you are using the right part number for that particular hub. This applies to cassette bodies too as there are different sizes for eight- and nine-speed, and XTR cassettes are of a better quality.

1 Remove the cassette using a chain whip and a cassette-removing tool. The chain whip prevents the cassette from turning, and should be positioned so that the chain on the tool can wrap around the sprocket enough to prevent it from spinning when you push on the wrench.

2 The lock ring threads into the cassette body and secures the sprockets. Because the cassette is integral to the drive, it needs to be tight. The serrated teeth pressed into the last sprocket and the underside of the lock ring prevent it from vibrating loose.

3 The first two or three cassette sprockets will be loose, so be careful not to drop them. Lay the wheel flat on the workbench and take the sprockets off one by one, placing them down in the order in which they came off the wheel.

4 Once the loose cassette sprockets and washers have been removed, the main cassette cluster can slide off. There is a series of slots cut into the cassette body. These are shaped so that the sprockets can only be returned the right way around.

5 Flip the hub over and work on the non-drive side. Remove the rubber cover and undo the lock nut. As with the front hub, leave the drive side intact to ensure that the spacing remains identical – this is especially important with the rear hub as uneven spacing can affect the chainline and the gear shifting.

6 As with the front hubs, set all the axle components to one side and clean the hub bearing surfaces. When the hub is cleaned, remove the cassette body with a 10 mm Allen key. The cassette body is usually factory fitted and tight, so you will need an appropriate Allen key (i.e. a long one). You may need to use a pipe for a little extra leverage to undo the bolt.

7 The bolt that retains the cassette body can be fully removed and the cassette body can be replaced if necessary. The cassette body is located on a spline on the side of the hub. Be careful not to lose the washer that sits on the inside of the body. Set the torque wrench to 34.3–49 Nm and tighten the bolt.

8 Grease and reset the bearings into the hub. 9 x $\frac{1}{4}$ inch bearings are usually required, but, as with the front hub, double-check that you are returning the same amount as you removed. It is impossible to detect damage to the surface of the bearings, so new ones must be used to ensure smooth running. Take your time and set the bearings in grease so that they are covered and the grease is worked in.

9 The grease will be enough to hold the bearings in place. Insert the axle, with the drive-side spacers and cones still in place, from the drive side. It is best to do this over the bench in case the bearings decide to escape.

10 Spin the non-drive side cone onto the axle and set the cone finger tight. Add any spacers and washers and finally the lock nut, then set the cones. This is harder with the rear hub because the drive-side cone is tucked into the cassette body. It is therefore far easier to do this job with the wheel secured in an axle vise, and some mechanics even adjust the hub when it is back in the bike. However, this requires experience. Lastly, return any rubber covers and you will then be able to reinstall the cassette.

11 Apply a thin layer of grease or anti-seize to the cassette body before you slide the cassette back into place. This will prevent the cassette body from rusting as water can get into the cassette very easily. If there is any corrosion on the body, use a fine wire brush to clean it off. A brass suede shoe brush is good to have in your tool kit for this type of job.

12 Lastly, replace the cassette cluster, the washers, the loose sprockets and the lock ring. Then tighten the lock ring to 35–50 Nm. You'll be surprised how tight this is, but the cassette bears a considerable load and needs to be checked for tightness regularly.

TIPS

· If you don't have a cassette-remover holding tool like the one pictured above, use a large or adjustable wrench. You will need to use the quick-release lever to prevent the tool from slipping. Some mechanics place the tool in a vise and use the chain whip only, but either way you will have to secure the remover to prevent it slipping and damaging the cassette lock ring.

· Cassette crackers are small portable tools that you can carry with you on the trail. You clamp them into the bike, then use the pedals and bike chain as your chain whip. Cassette crackers also fit Shimano disc brake lock rings, so they are a very effective emergency tool and well worth having in your tool kit.

· Cassette bodies can be soaked in release agent (paraffin or diesel fuel) overnight to rejuvenate the internals. This will not cure long-term problems, but will shift the muck from the mechanism and can keep it going for a little longer.

· If you thoroughly degrease and clean your cassette regularly and replace your chain every 1,200–1,800 miles, it will last a lot longer – sometimes up to five times longer than a cassette that is neglected. Remove and degrease the cassette whenever it gets full of dirt or chain muck. See pages 43–45 for more on bike cleaning.

Cartridge hubs

The following method for fitting new bearings in hubs with cartridge units is fairly straightforward. Each manufacturer will have its own tools and bearings. Unlike adjustable cup and cone style hubs, cartridge bearing hubs rely on a sealed bearing unit that can be removed and replaced. The bearings are set into a hardened steel cartridge that press-fits into the hub shell or freewheel body. This unit is packed with grease and sealed with plastic or labyrinth seals. The quality is determined by the number of bearings and amount of grease packed into them. Once the bearing is pushed into the hub, the axle can be pushed tightly into the bearings. This gives you a smooth spinning feel, as there is less chance of overtightening the bearing with lock nuts and cones.

The obvious advantage of sealed bearings is that they require less adjustment and servicing than standard cup and cone bearings. However, they are only as good as the quality of bearings and standard of engineering of the hub shells. A cartridge hub at the cheaper end of the range may have push-fit covers and less sealing than a Shimano cup and cone hub.

Sealed bearings do not like side loads and can be easily damaged, so always treat them with care and always use the manufacturer's recommended tools to remove them.

Tools required:
- **plastic mallet**
- **bearing fitting dies**
- **Allen keys**
- **cleaning kit**
- **grease**
- **cone wrench**

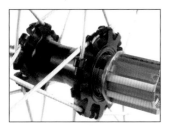

 The spacers at the end of each side of the axle are either push-fit or locked into place with a threaded lock ring. Sometimes a grub screw can lock them in place. The ones shown here require an Allen key and a cone wrench to undo the cassette-retaining spacer.

 This non-drive-side spacer threads onto the axle end. Many (like Hope) are a simple push-on fitting. The key here is the quality of the fit between the axle and the bearing, as this is what takes the strain. Oversize axles are a good idea with sealed bearings as they can handle much more abuse and tend to twist less under drive.

With the spacers and lock nuts removed, the cassette body can be taken off. On most cartridge hubs the cassette will be a push-fit secured by the drive-side spacer. However, some, like this Bontrager wheel, use a Shimano-type freewheel that is bolted to the hub body. You will need a 10 mm Allen key to remove this.

 Push out the old cartridge bearings. This Bontrager wheel's axle has to be tapped out with a plastic mallet. Once one side has been removed, the cartridge will pop out, still attached to the axle.

5 This Bontrager hub has a bolt-on cassette body and is removed in the same way as a Shimano hub (see step 3) with a 10 mm Allen key. You can see the collar that holds the cartridge bearing. This needs to be cleaned thoroughly before a new bearing can be installed.

6 The remaining bearing on the axle can be tapped off by placing the axle in a die. This allows you to use the axle as a drift to remove the remaining bearing on the other side of the hub. To replace the bearing you will have to place it on top of the die and tap the axle back in. When it is flush to the shoulder in the center of the axle, it is ready to be re-installed to the hub.

7 The new bearings can be replaced. All sealed bearings have a code number and can be bought at most engineering suppliers or your local bike shop.

8 Use an appropriate die to seat the new bearings into the hub. They are a tight fit, but must be installed gently so as not to damage the bearing unit or the seals. Press in the new bearings with care. Put some grease around the outside of the bearing and place it square onto the hub. Use an insertion tool that is the same size as the outer part of the bearing. Any side load onto the plastic seal part of the bearing will ruin it. Tap the bearing home.

9 Most cartridge bearing hubs have their own type of cassette. They usually pull off once the lock rings and spacers have been removed. Inside the hub is a series of teeth and on the cassette body are three sprung pawls. These pawls engage with the teeth when you pedal and 'click' around freely when you stop pedaling. The hub pictured here has one circular spring that holds the pawls in place.

10 Here you can see the serrated part inside the hub. This needs to be completely cleaned out and lightly greased before you replace the rebuilt cassette body.

11 Carefully remove the pawls and clean all the dirty grease off the cassette body. Use a toothbrush to clean out all the pawl indentations and spring channels.

12 The cassette shown here has a single circular spring, so the pawls need to be set in grease and then have the spring replaced over them. This does take time as it's quite tricky. Many hubs have springs for individual pawls. If these fail they will need replacing as they can get stuck into the serrated parts and ruin the freewheel.

13 Use a lightweight grease on the freewheels. Heavy grease tends to drag inside the hub, which can make the chain sag. To replace the cassette body you will need to push the pawls into the cassette body so it can fit into the hub. Some hubs supply a tool for this. Once the pawls are tucked away, the cassette body should pop into place. Double-check that it rotates freely before you rebuild the rest of the hub.

TIPS – SEALED BEARINGS

- With care, the seals can be removed with a scalpel blade and the old grease flushed out with degreaser. Use a grease gun to inject fresh grease into the bearings inside the collars.
- Avoid solvent-based lubricants on sealed bearing hubs as they can damage the seals and flush out the grease from the bearings.

9

Headsets

The headset is a very simple component and the unit is therefore easy to service. A well-prepared head tube and a properly fitted headset will help the unit last longer. Even the cheaper headsets on the market can last a long time if your bike is properly prepared and the unit is serviced regularly. The system consists of two bearing races positioned at either end of the head tube. The races run in these bearings and are trapped by the fork at one end and the stem at the other. The stem clamps the system together and prevents it from coming loose.

SUSPENSION AND STEERING

Headset parts

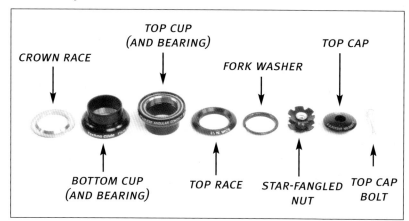

CROWN RACE

TOP CUP
(AND BEARING)

FORK WASHER

TOP CAP

BOTTOM CUP
(AND BEARING)

TOP RACE

STAR-FANGLED
NUT

TOP CAP
BOLT

Types of headsets

1 inch or 1 1/8 inch?

Bicycle fork steerers were 1 inch for many years, before the headset forks were threaded into the headset, but the threaded type is now very rare. Most mountain bikes now have a 1$\frac{1}{8}$ inch headset; some downhill bikes may have a 1$\frac{1}{2}$ inch fork, but these are also rare. Generally speaking, shorter, slimmer head tubes do put more strain on the bearings than long ones.

Integrated headsets

Integrated headsets have come over to mountain bikes from road bikes. With integrated headsets, the bearings are pushed directly into the frame. The factory will have fitted these and the quality of the frame building is always going to dictate how good this will be. In my experience, standard head tubes are better because they allow easier servicing and can be easier to find replacements for.

Headset cups

Headset cups can be made from steel, aluminum or titanium. Stainless steel cups are becoming popular with downhillers and jump riders, as they have extra-long inserts to support the head tube and prevent the unit loosening, and also last longer. Aluminum cups are still the most popular and titanium cups are lightweight but quite pricey. There is one brand that stands apart from the rest – Chris King. I have had King headsets that have lasted longer than frames – they are superb.

Basic headset adjustment

1 To check the headset, apply the front brake and rock the bike backward and forward. You will feel or hear a slight knocking if the unit is loose. If you have been running the unit loose for a while, the chances are that the bearings will need replacing; riding with a loose headset will batter the bearings and ruin the surfaces in the unit.

2 Undo the two bolts on the side of the stem. These bolts clamp the stem to the top of the steerer and also keep the headset unit complete. The one pictured here has a cut-away section at the rear, so you can see the shiny steel fork steerer it is clamping on to.

3 Once you have loosened the bolts, tighten the top cap slightly (or preload it) to take up any play in the system. You will only need a small nip to tighten the unit (to around 3 Nm). If you are removing the top cap and fork as well as the headset, be aware that the fork will be free to fall out once the clamp is undone and the top cap removed. If you are just servicing the headset, remove the bars and unhook the brakes so that the forks can be removed and set aside.

4 The bearings will be either a sealed cartridge or ball bearings, as shown here. Both systems are good, but the advantage with loose bearings is that they can be stripped out and regreased. The advantage with cartridge-type bearings is that they can be completely replaced. If the bearings are wearing out regularly, the cups could be out of line in the frame and they will therefore need to be refitted.

5 Once you have serviced the bearings, the forks can be reinstalled. Make sure that you return all the seals the right way up and that you grease the bearings and insert them into the cups the right way around. Do not leave the forks in the bike without returning the stem, even if the friction in the seals appears to be enough to hold them in place. I managed to break a toe doing this as I let go of the bike to turn around and pick up the stem and the fork fell out on to my foot . . . now I always wear work boots to fix a bike.

6 There should be a gap between the top of the steerer and the top of the stem of approximately 2–3 mm. The gap shouldn't be any bigger than this as the stem bolts must be able to tighten over the steerer. If the bolts are above the height of the steerer, the stem will be distorted and will not be tightened to the correct torque figure. The problem isn't just that you might pull the bars off, but the stem will also loosen over time and damage the bearings.

7 When you replace the top cap, check that the bottom of the top cap doesn't snag on the top of the steerer. If it does, place an extra spacer on top of the stem to give a little more space.

8 Most stems have two clamp bolts, one on either side, so that the stem will not be pulled over to one side as you tighten the bolts. It is critical that you do not over- or undertighten these bolts. Retighten the stem clamp bolts to the recommended torque setting – 10–12 Nm per bolt is adequate and will mean that the bars will still twist in the event of a crash.

9 Before refitting the handlebars, check that there are no sharp edges around the stem clamp. Also check that you have the right diameter bars and stem. Standard mountain bike stems are 25.4 mm and road bike stems are usually 26.0 mm, but the latest size ('Oversize') is 31.8 mm, for both road and mountain bike stems. Most decent handlebar stems, such as the one pictured here, have slightly beveled edges. Put a dab of grease or copper slip on the stem bolts before replacing them to prevent them from seizing.

10 Replace the front section of the bar clamp. Number the bolts 1–4 clockwise, then tighten them alternately (e.g., 1–3–2–4) and to 6–7 Nm. Do not overtighten the bolts or tighten them too quickly – make sure you reach the desired torque setting gradually. Line the handlebars up (the one pictured here has a handy line for your reference) and make sure that you have positioned them centrally. See pages 91–92 for more on handlebar setup.

11 Once you have tightened the stem, check that there is an equal gap at the top and bottom between the clamping sections. If there is a difference, tighten or loosen the stem bolts until they match. This is critical, as it will ensure that there is an equal force on each bolt and that the bar is properly clamped. This is especially important with carbon bars and lightweight aluminum ones.

12 Check that the bars are straight and that the stem is tight. Line the bars up with the front hub. You can hold the wheel between your legs and line the bars up by twisting them. You may need to loosen the stem bolts slightly to make this possible.

13 Finally, recheck that the headset is adjusted properly. First, check for play (as in step 1). Then pick up the bike's front end in one hand, just behind the head tube. The bars should turn or 'flop' to one side very easily. If the bars stay put, facing forward, the headset is too tight and the bearings are binding up and you will need to readjust it. If the headset remains tight and you have tried resetting the stem bolts, it's likely that one of the bearings or weather seals has been inserted the wrong way, so check this and retighten.

Stack height

I have already mentioned that headsets come in a variety of different sizes (1 inch, 1 1/8 inch and 1/2 inch), but each manufacturer makes them with a different stack height too. Stack height is the amount of space that the cups take up on the steerer (A + B). If you are fitting a new headset, make sure that you buy a similar make or one with the same stack height. If the stack is too high, the stem won't have enough steerer to hold on to.

Remember that most forks will be ruined if you cut the steerer too short as they can't be replaced easily, so always double-check your measurements before you cut.

Fitting headsets and forks

To install headsets correctly, you need to prepare your frame carefully and to have some specialist tools. Often, the bike shop will fit the forks and therefore do this preparation work for you, but if you need to do it yourself, it is important to follow the steps below – your bike will ride better and last longer if you do.

Titanium frames will usually not require the facing and cleaning out process, as this will have been done in the factory when the frame was made. Carbon frames will also usually have been faced properly. As always, consult the manufacturer's instructions or ask your local dealer if you are unsure.

Tools required:
- sharp hacksaw
- fork cutting guide
- star-fangled setting tool
- permanent marker pen and ruler
- Allen keys
- metal half-round file
- cup-removing tool
- mallet
- crown race removing tool
- headset press tool

1 Remove and replace the headset if necessary. Check that the travel matches your new fork or, if the new fork has longer travel, that the frame's geometry can handle it. Old headset cups can be removed with a cup-removing tool like this one, which splays out inside the head tube and ensures a snug fit on the inside of the cups. It rests on top of the cups and allows you to tap it out with equal force. Using a long screwdriver is not an option as it can damage the inside of the frame and ruin the cups.

2 Tap the cup-removing tool with a mallet to remove the cups. With some smaller head tubes it can be tricky to get the tool to fit properly, as the jaws can be restricted by the other race. So be careful and make sure you wrap a cloth around the cup to prevent it pinging off around the workshop.

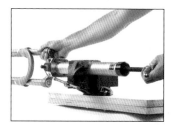

3 Remove the old crown race. The crown race is a very delicate component and can also be slightly smaller than the crown of most suspension forks, which makes it very difficult to remove – unless you have a crown race removing tool. You can remove some crown races by tapping them with a plastic mallet and a suitably soft drift, but it is far better to use a crown race removing tool as it won't scratch the forks and damage the crown.

4 The tool pictured here is a dual-purpose cutter: it faces the head tube and also cuts the inside of the tube at the same time, making sure that the headset cups are inserted squarely into the tube. The top and the bottom of the tube are faced to ensure that the cups are parallel, so they don't work against each other and wear out quickly. It will remove any rust or paint on the tube and also make sure the cups are a perfect fit.

5 When you have faced the tube, it will look perfectly flat and shiny like this one and the headset cups will fit squarely into the tube. Clean out all the leftover metal shavings and particles from the facing process from the inside and grease the top and bottom faces with some anti-seize grease. Grease the inner parts of the cups too, and check to see which is the top and which is the bottom (the logos are usually a dead giveaway).

6 The headset press tool simply forces the cups into the head tube. Do not try to install a headset with a hammer as it will not work; a headset press tool will do the job in seconds and will prevent any damage to the frame or headset components. Remove any seals from the cups as they may get damaged as the cup is pressed in. Insert the cup so that it is straight and cannot distort as you force it in with the tool – the cups usually have a beveled edge to guide them into the tube. Line up the logos too so the front end looks tidy, which is why it is best to do one cup at a time. Some cups have grease guard ports, which should face to the side so you can get to them easily.

7 When you have installed the bottom cup, the top cup can go in. The tool has a variety of dies that fit different sized cups. Make sure that you use one that fits well but not too snugly as the force on the tool can seize onto the aluminum cup and ruin it. You will find that the cups will be easier to install if the head tube has been cut and faced. Finally, inspect the cups closely to check that they are flush with the tube (hold the bike up to the light and see if there are any gaps).

8 It is best to measure the old fork steerer with a ruler first and then compare it with the old forks once you've marked them. Mark the steerer with a permanent marker pen as you will have to insert the forks into the head tube before it is cut. Do not scratch a mark with a file or hacksaw blade as it could be wrong and the scratch will act as a stress riser and weaken the steerer.

9 Next, fit the fork crown race. Most suspension forks will have factory-cut crowns, but some need facing for a perfect fit – there is a workshop tool to do this job if necessary. This tool is used to knock the crown race onto the crown – make sure that the adaptor is a good fit to the race and remove any rubber or plastic seals before you do this as they can be damaged. If you don't have a crown race tool, consider buying an headset unit with a split race. This is a good idea for suspension forks with large crowns, which present problems when trying to remove the race. These usually come with sealed cartridge bearing units, as they need to retain the bearings rather than running the bearings directly on top of it.

10 Assemble the complete system at this point to check you have the steerer at the right length. Although you may not want to cut the steerer twice, it's better to allow for more spacers if you are unsure how high you want your bars. If I am assembling a bike for someone else, I always leave 30 mm of spacers under the stem so that the rider can decide. The steerer can always be cut again after a test ride. Cut the steerer to length using a sharp new hacksaw blade, holding the steerer in a cutting guide to stop the blade wandering as you cut. It is essential that the cut is square to ensure that the stem fits properly and the star nut can be installed easily. If you are cutting a carbon-fiber steerer, wear a facemask. File off any burrs on the outside and inside of the steerer tube with a half-round file. Take care not to scratch the steerer and make sure that the edges of the tube will not scratch the inside of the stem when you replace it. The inside has to be clear so that the top cap nut can be easily inserted inside the tube.

11 The star-fangled nut is the fixed part of the system and allows the top cap to fasten down on the headset stack, and also allows you to adjust out any play in the system. They are not recommended for carbon-fiber steerers and they may be difficult to fit to some aluminum steerers with thicker tube walls. Use a star-fangled setting tool, as pictured here, and you can't fail to get it set straight in the steerer.

12 Once inserted, the star-fangled nut is very hard to remove as it fits by wedging itself into the inside of the tube. This scratches the tube, so removing the nut can make a big mess of both the nut and the steerer. If the star-fangled nut is damaged or seized, simply knock it farther down the steerer and fit a replaceable wedge.

13 Alternatively, you can use a replaceable top cap and wedge. I prefer to use one of these top caps, which has a separate wedge that is inserted and tightened into the steerer with an Allen key. These are safer and can be refitted, which is really important if you don't have a star-fangled nut setting tool. They also cannot damage the inside of the steerer tube. But, best of all, they are also less likely to rust and seize as you can remove them and clean them up.

Suspension

The basic idea behind mountain bike suspension is to help isolate the rider from small to medium bumps, reducing rider fatigue and enhancing the overall mountain bike experience. Suspension also improves bike control by allowing the two wheels to track the terrain, maintaining traction. So the key is to keep the suspension supple, whatever type of riding you do – if the suspension is too soft, your bike will use up the travel quickly and possibly damage the internals, and if it is too hard it will make the bike bounce off rough stuff like a pogo stick.

In this book we won't be going into the nuances of each particular suspension configuration, as there are too many of them and they are constantly changing in terms of design and setup. So instead we will concentrate on the fundamentals of any suspension setup: damping and spring rate. *Damping* controls how quickly the shock or fork compresses or rebounds, while the *spring rate* suspends the rider and determines how much the suspension compresses under the combined weight of the bike and rider.

The majority of mountain bikes are either air or coil sprung. Determining which spring your rear suspension uses is easy as the spring is external, so you will be able to see either a coil spring or an air canister with a Schraeder valve. Suspension forks are trickier as the springs are housed inside the stanchions (upper legs). To identify which system your fork uses, consult the owner's manual or inspect the dials on the fork crown. See pages 135–39 for more on suspension forks.

Setting the sag

The most important setting on any mountain bike suspension system is the sag. This is the amount by which the suspension compresses under the combined weight of the bike and rider. So you must set the sag before you ride the bike and check it regularly for optimum performance. Running at 15–25 per cent of the available travel of a fork or shock in sag is essential as this lets the suspension absorb holes as well as bumps, enabling the wheel to hug the ground. The same basic principles apply to forks and shocks, but we will deal with both separately as the techniques for setting the sag vary slightly.

Rear suspension unit

Whatever design you prefer, your bike's suspension system is only as good as the elements that control the travel and the response to trail conditions. The latest generation of shocks are now 'trail sensitive' in that they are controlled by rider input to the pedals and weight distribution across the bike, rather than the rider having to fiddle with knobs and dials. Remote lockout levers have made cross-country suspension bikes climb hills without bobbing or soaking up energy, and they are fast becoming the top choice for Enduro riders and racers. Rear shocks are sealed units and are best serviced by experts, so send them away to those who know best as some require compression and specialist tooling to get them apart.

Forks

1 If there isn't already an O-ring on the stanchion (upper tube), wrap a small zip tie around the leg. Slide this (or the O-ring) down the fork leg until it touches the fork wiper seal.

2 Prop yourself up against a wall with your elbow, or ask for help to hold the bike upright, and sit on the bike in the normal riding position. If you've compressed the fork a lot when getting on the bike, you will need to reach down and reset the O-ring. You are looking to spread your weight without bouncing on the saddle or pedals.

3 Being careful not to compress the fork further, climb off the bike and measure the sag directly from the fork leg. Sag should be between 15 and 25 per cent of the total travel available, keeping in mind that the total travel will always be slightly less than the amount of stanchion showing. For example, on an 80 mm fork you should look for sag of 12–20 mm.

4 If you have air-sprung forks, simply increase the air pressure to reduce the amount of sag, or decrease the air pressure to increase the sag.

5 Coil-sprung forks will normally have a dial on the fork crown that is used to preload the spring. If you find that the fork sags too much with the preload fully on, you'll need to install a firmer spring. If it sags too little with no preload, you'll need to fit a softer spring.

6 When the sag is set correctly, if you find that the fork bottoms out (goes through all of the available travel) more than a couple of times every time you ride, you'll need to increase the compression damping. If the fork does not have adjustable compression damping, your only option will be to increase the spring rate (steps 4 and 5).

TIP

You can decrease the air pressure by pressing the release valve on the shock pump.

Coil-sprung shock

The trusty coil shock may be heavier than its air-sprung equivalent, but many riders find that the extra weight is a small price to pay for the buttery smooth action and inherent reliability. Unlike an air-sprung shock, a coil spring is not a 'one size fits all' affair. The preload adjuster allows a small degree of fine-tuning, but the best performance is achieved when the spring weight offers the correct amount of sag with minimal preloading – typically two turns of the preload collar. To determine the correct setup, follow these steps:

1 Wind off the compression and rebound damping adjusters. In the fully open position the shock should rebound quickly and compress easily.

2 Unscrew the preload collar to the point just before the spring starts to rattle. Then wind it back two full turns.

3 Read the number on the side of the spring to find the spring rate. This is measured in pounds per inch, so a spring rate of 450 lbs means that it takes a force of 450 lbs to compress the spring by 1 inch.

4 Measure the sag. The easiest way to do this on a coil shock is to first measure the unweighted eye-to-eye distance of the shock. Next, sit on the saddle in normal riding gear and measure the weighted eye-to-eye distance. Subtracting the second measurement from the first will tell you how much the shock has compressed.

5 Typically, sag should measure one quarter to one third of the entire shock stroke. So, a shock with a 2-inch stroke should have approximately half to two thirds of an inch in sag. Too much sag and you need a heavier spring (bigger number); too little and you'll need a lighter spring (smaller number). Dial in the rebound and compression adjusters. Note that the settings will be different if you have changed the weight of the spring.

Air-sprung shock

While air-sprung shocks can't quite match the plushness of coil-sprung units, they are lighter. Also, because the air spring is adjustable (more air pressure increases the spring rate and less decreases it), there is no messing around with springs – all you need is a good shock pump. Before you set the sag, set any compression, rebound or pedal platforming to minimum.

1 A good starting point for any air shock is your body weight in pounds. So, if you weigh 150 lbs, inflate the positive air chamber to 150 PSI.

2 Push the shock O-ring up the shock body so that it butts up against the air canister.

3 Propping yourself up against a wall with your elbow, sit on the bike in your normal riding position. If you've compressed the shock a lot when getting on the bike, you will need to reach down and reset the O-ring.

4 Being careful not to compress the shock further, climb off the bike and measure the sag directly from the shock body.

5 Run between 15 and 25 per cent of the available travel in sag. So, if your shock has a 1/2-inch stroke, start with 3/8 inch in sag. Inflate the shock to reduce the amount of sag or reduce the air pressure to increase the sag – it's that easy. As with forks, if you find that you bottom the shock easily, increase the air pressure and reduce the amount of sag. Alternatively, if the shock has a compression damping adjustment, increase the compression damping to prevent the shock from bottoming.

TIPS

- If you are running on minimum preload, wrap a piece of insulation or PTFE tape around the threads of the shock body as shown in the photograph to stop the preload collar backing off.
- Rotate the spring so that its tail isn't on the open section of the C-clip, as this can cause the spring to click.
- Replacement springs don't come cheap, but some service centers offer exchanges at reduced rates.

Using sag setting to fine-tune bike geometry

The amount of sag you run affects the geometry of the bike. So, if you find that the bottom bracket is too low or the head angle is too slack, run slightly less sag in the rear shock to raise the bottom bracket and steepen the head angle. Alternatively, if the bottom bracket is overly high or the head angle too steep, increase the amount of sag to counter this.

If you're riding steep, technical terrain where the switchbacks drop away suddenly, you may want to increase the spring rate in the fork. This reduces the amount of sag so that you ride higher in the travel. Not only will this slacken the head angle slightly, making the bike more stable at speed, but it will also stop the fork from diving as much, making those slow, tight, rocky switchbacks all the easier to clean.

TIPS

Platform damping can affect the sag setting, so if you make changes to your level of platform damping – especially if it's controlled by the internal floating piston (IFP) pressure as found on Manitou and Progressive shocks – always check the sag.

Some shocks have bodies that are considerably longer than the stroke of the shock. This can lead to a false sag reading, so always deflate the shock then fully compress it to determine the true shock stroke.

Adjusting the rebound damping

With the sag set, the next step to achieving the perfect suspension setup is to fine-tune the rebound damping. While air and coil springs suspend the rider, it's the oils and valves inside the shock that control the energy released by the spring. Specifically, rebound damping controls how fast the shock or fork returns (rebounds) to the sag position. Too much damping and the suspension will return slowly and won't be ready for the next hit; not enough damping causes the suspension to spring back uncontrollably.

Shocks and forks have a massive range of adjustment so it is very easy to get the rebound setting wrong. And because the majority of weight on a full suspension bike is supported by the rear suspension, it is the most important thing to get right. Before adjusting the damping, follow the steps outlined on pages 130–33 for setting the correct amount of sag. With the sag sorted and the rebound adjuster fully out, ride off a medium-sized curb in the seated position. You should be able to feel the shock oscillating about the sag position beneath you on impact. Increase the rebound damping by a click and repeat. When the shock settles to the sag position within two cycles, you're ready to ride.

As a rule, less rebound damping makes the bike springier and increases the sensitivity of the suspension to small bumps, while increasing the rebound damping stops the bike bucking on drops and big hits but reduces some of the sensitivity. The steps outlined above are just a guideline to get you started. If you find that on the trail the bike bucks too much and feels uncontrolled, gradually increase the rebound damping. On the other hand, if the suspension seems to pack down and isn't responsive to smaller bumps, reduce the amount of rebound damping. It's also worth noting that suspension feedback into the drivetrain is less noticeable with increased damping. Ultimately, there is no ideal setting, so experiment and find out what works best for you.

Care and regular checks for forks

Most riders neglect their forks, but the suspension is a moving part that is exposed to the elements so regular cleaning and lubrication are essential. Just like the drivetrain, neglect will cause premature wear and diminished performance, often resulting in irreparable damage.

Anatomy of a suspension fork

Steerer tube

The steerer tube is a butted aluminum or steel threadless tube that connects the fork to the frame via the headset and is usually $1^1/_8$ inch in diameter. 1.5 inch is an oversized head tube/fork standard that allows manufacturers to make lightweight long-travel single crown forks without compromising strength.

Crown

Fork crowns are forged or cast and are often hollow to save weight. The steerer tube is normally press-fitted into the crown, as are the stanchions (see below).

Stanchions

All telescopic suspension forks have stanchions (upper tubes). Diameters vary from 28.6 mm on XC forks to 40 mm on some downhill forks. Aluminum is the favored material to keep weight down, and stanchions normally have a hardened surface coating to reduce stiction and wear.

Dust seals

Also called wiper seals, these are the primary defense in keeping contaminants out of the forks. The improved quality of dust seals has made boots redundant.

Oil seals

These are hidden beneath the dust seals and keep the oil inside the fork.

Front fork with lockout

Front suspension has been a regular fixture on mountain bikes for the last ten years, and it's actually pretty rare to see a bike with rigid forks these days. Like rear suspension units, the new style of fork is far more sophisticated and, as with most high-tech mountain bike components, servicing them is more prevention than cure. The servicing of modern forks, especially those with lockout and damping features, is best carried out by experienced technicians – trying to strip forks without instructions and a set of sophisticated tools is asking for trouble. However, most of the budget forks can be looked after at home easily enough.

Bushings

Most forks have upper and lower bushings (bearings) in each leg to guide the stanchions into the lowers.

Lowers

Normally cast from magnesium to minimize unsprung mass, the fork lowers are the bits that have to move up and down over the bumps and include the brace, which prevents the fork legs from moving independently.

Dropouts

This is where the wheel is secured. The dropouts can be either quick release or 20 mm bolt-through. Quick-release dropouts have safety tabs to stop the front wheel from falling out if the quick release accidentally comes undone. That's why you have to open the quick release and actually unwind it to remove the front wheel.

Fork maintenance

As with any moving part, fork maintenance consists of cleaning and lubrication. So, after every ride clean the stanchions and wiper seals, paying particular attention to the area between the fork brace and the seal. Add a drop of oil and massage it in by pumping the forks a few times.

Tools required:
- **2 mm Allen key**
- **8 mm Allen key**
- **syringe**
- **Simi-bath fluid**
- **11 mm socket**

Manitou forks

Early Manitou forks use a micro-lube system, where grease is injected into the fork through ports on the back of the lower legs. But Manitou has recently switched to a Simi-bath lubrication system with 16 cc of oil slopping around in each of the lower legs to keep everything running smoothly. Over time, the oil breaks down and eventually weeps out through the wiper seals. Here we show you how to top up the lubrication fluids in the latest generation of Manitou forks.

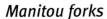

1 On forks with rapid travel adjust or wind-down, make sure that you switch the travel to the longest setting. Then turn the bike upside down, exposing the bottom of the fork lowers. Using a 2 mm Allen key, remove any adjusters (making a note of their orientation) and place to one side.

2 If the fork does not have a rapid travel adjuster, you will see an 11 mm bolt at the bottom of the left leg (rider's perspective). Remove this bolt with an 11 mm socket, turning it counter-clockwise.

3 Insert an 8 mm Allen key into the right leg (rider's perspective) but do not unscrew it. The Allen head is attached directly to the rebound damper shaft and must be screwed into the fork (clockwise) to release the lowers.

4 Slide the lowers up by about 2 inches to disengage the damper and spring shafts. Using a syringe, inject 16 cc of Simi-bath oil into each leg.

5 Press the lower legs down onto the inner leg assembly (stanchions) until the damper shafts make contact with the casting. Using the 8 mm Allen key, turn the damper shaft counter-clockwise into the lower leg.

6 Install the damper rod and adjuster if applicable. Install the spring rod bolt and torque to 2–3 Nm using an 11 mm socket. Install the rapid travel adjuster if applicable. Upright the bike and check that the forks function as normal.

Fork types

Dual-crown forks

As the name suggests, these have two crowns. The stanchions extend up through the lower crown and are bolted to the steerer tube with a sliding upper crown. Although heavier than normal forks, the dual-crown fork design is considerably stiffer and a lot stronger than a conventional single-crown fork.

Upside-down (inverted) forks

With upside-down forks, the stanchions are the lower legs and there is no brace. A bolt-through axle and associated dropouts are used to stop the legs from moving independently, but as a rule upside-down forks are not as stiff as conventional designs. Advantages of the design include reduced unsprung mass and excellent tire clearance.

Fox forks

Fox recommends that you lube the foam O-ring under the wiper seal after every 25 hours of riding. This is a basic service, but it will make the forks last longer and prevent damage to the internals.

Tools required:
· **small flat-blade screwdriver**
· **large flat-blade screwdriver**
· **Fox suspension fluid**
· **clean rags**

1 Use a small flat-blade screwdriver to pry the seals from the lower legs of the fork. The fork seals have small notches to make this easier. Fox recommends that the tip of the screwdriver be covered with tape to protect the paint on the fork. Go one step further and wrap clean rags around the stanchions to prevent them from getting scratched.

2 Once the seals are loose, remove the rags and slide the seals all the way up to the crown. Take the same rags and wrap them around the junction of the upper and lower legs to stop dirt getting into the fork.

3 Use another rag to clean the outside edge of the seals. Remove all the dirt and inspect the seals for damage like cracks or scratches in the surface.

4 Remove the rags from the fork legs and inspect the foam O-rings inside the lower legs.

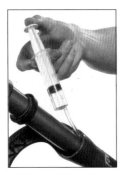

5 The seals should be free of dirt and soaked in oil. If the foam O-rings are dry, use a few drops of Fox suspension fluid to soak them. Then wipe the upper tubes clean and slide the seals back down onto the lower legs.

6 Press the seals in using a large, covered flatblade screwdriver, starting between the fork brace and the stanchions and working your way around to the back of the fork.

7 Check that the seals are firmly seated against the fork lowers and compress the fork several times to check that everything is okay.

FOX TIP

Store your bike upside down to keep the upper bushing and foam O-ring soaked in oil, ready for your next ride. But remember to cycle the fork several times when you upright the bike to recharge the damper with oil.

Trouble shooting

The fork is rocking
Check that the headset is tight (see pages 124–26) as the bushing may be worn. Have the fork inspected by a professional suspension-tuning center.

The fork is topping out
Increase the rebound damping. If this doesn't cure the problem, the internals may be damaged.

The fork is bottoming out
The spring rate may be too soft, or there may be insufficient compression damping. If the sag is correct then you need to increase the damping.

The fork feels harsh
The spring could be too firm, or you may have too much compression damping resulting in a 'spike'. If the fork doesn't have an external compression adjuster, try using a lighter-weight oil in the fork.

The fork rebounds too quickly
Increase the rebound damping and, if the fork doesn't have an external rebound adjuster, try using a lighter-weight oil in the fork, assuming that the fork isn't friction damped.

After compression the fork takes ages to return to the sag position
Completely back off the rebound damping and, if that doesn't cure the problem, get it checked out at an authorized service center.

The fork action is notchy
This is probably due to stiction (static friction). Strip and clean the fork as per the manufacturer's instructions, or have it serviced at a recognized service center.

TIPS
- Brake and gear outer cables can cut into a fork crown after a couple of rides. Cover any contact areas with protective patches or shorten the cables so that they don't rub.
- Wrap a zip tie around one of the stanchions to make it easier to set the sag. This will also check that the forks are working and you are actually getting full travel.
- When suspension forks were first introduced on mountain bikes, most sported boots or gators. Their function was twofold: they kept dirt out and prevented the stanchions (upper legs) from getting scratched. But the improved quality of wiper seals – and fashion – spelled the end for the trusty boot. You can add neoprene gators in really wet weather for extra protection, but they can keep the fork damp, so it's better still to strip and service the forks after prolonged wet use.

Rear shock maintenance

If you've got a full suspension bike, it doesn't take long to figure out that with all those moving parts something is bound to wear out. Invariably, the first thing to go is the DU bushing – that's the small collar in either end of the shock. Virtually all rear shocks, regardless of whether or not they are air- or coil-sprung, are fixed to the frame using DU bushings and aluminum fitting hardware. Shock manufacturers like Manitou, Fox, RockShox and Progressive Suspension all use universal eyelet dimensions and the bushings are designed to be perishable so that the inexpensive bushing wears, rather than expensive shock unit.

Shock and rider location both determine how quickly the bushing will wear out. On the whole, the bushings on shocks that are positioned in front of the seat tube last longer, as they are not in the firing line of mud being flung off the rear wheel. Also, if you live in a dry, dusty climate, chances are that the bushings could last for years.

Tools required:
- Allen keys
- 10 mm wrench
- DU bushing tool

Checking for and replacing a worn bushing

1 Before rushing out to buy the necessary tools and replacement bushings, check that the shock mounting bolts are actually tight. If you discover a bolt that isn't fully tightened, remove it, apply a small amount of Loctite to the threads and re-fit it.

2 With the shock secured, apply a small amount of downward pressure on the back portion of the saddle, then lift the saddle up ever so slightly, keeping the rear wheel on the ground at all times.

3 If there is a small knock, similar to a loose headset, then one or both of the bushings are worn. If you watch the bushings while rocking the saddle you should be able to see the movement and determine which one needs replacing.

4 Remove the shock from the frame using the appropriate Allen keys or wrenches.

5 If the DU bushing is worn, you should have no problem removing the alloy shock mounts. If they don't come out easily, clamp them in the soft jaws of a vise and wiggle them out. All Fox bushings are supplied with new fitting kits as both items tend to wear together, so don't worry about damaging the old hardware.

6 Slide the thin end of the male portion of the bushing tool through the shock eyelet.

7 Next, slide the tapered end of the female portion of the tool over the thin end of the male tool.

8 Place both ends of the tool in a vise and slowly compress until the worn bushing pops out.

9 Now, place a fresh bushing onto the thin end of the male tool and flip the female portion of the tool over so that the tapered end is in contact with the vise. Press in the new bushing.

10 Fit the new shock spacers and reinstall the shock.

TIPS

· When unbolting the shock, support the frame (or the rear wheel if the bike is in a stand) to stop the bike collapsing or overextending as this could damage the shock or frame. An old toe strap is good for this.

· Fit small O-rings between the DU bushings and fitting hardware to reduce dirt buildup. If you grease the bushing, wipe away any excess grease as it will retain dirt and accelerate wear. Have your shock serviced annually to maximize performance and longevity.

Troubleshooting

The shock is losing air
Check that the valve body is tight in the air canister and that the valve core is also tight.

The shock is topping out
Increase the amount of rebound damping. If the shock still tops out, take it to an authorized dealer for inspection.

There is an excessive amount of oil on the shock shaft (coil) or body (air)
Clean and inspect the seal. If the leaking persists, the shock will need servicing.

My shock is making slurping noises
The oil has become emulsified, that is gas and oil are mixed together, which will result in inconsistent damping. Return the shock for servicing.

The shock is packed down
Wind the rebound damping fully off (counter-clockwise). If this does not cure the problem, have the shock inspected at a service center.

Warning!
Do not attempt to dismantle shock units at home, as most shocks are charged with gas and dismantling them could result in serious injury. Always have your shock serviced at an authorized service center. And, as always: read the manual!

10

Frame preparation

Building a bike from scratch is a hugely rewarding process. However, you will only be able to do it properly, and it will only save you money, if you have the right tools. Much of the following chapter relies on specialist tools that only a bike shop will have access to. However, if you are buying a new frame to build up yourself, consider these steps before you part with any money. A good shop will fit bottom brackets, forks and headsets for you if you buy them from the same place, so it's always worth asking. Remember that a well-prepared frame is a solid foundation for both the components and the rider.

FRAME

Frame alignment

Frame alignment is the first step to building your perfect bike. This is easier to ascertain on a hardtail than it is on a full suspension bike. The head tube and seat tube have to be in line in order for the bike to handle properly, and the rear dropouts have to be positioned so that they hold the rear wheel directly behind the front wheel. This is called frame track. Crashing can cause invisible damage to mountain bikes, so track should be regularly checked out. Use some of the following steps as they will help you identify problems and damage. This assessment is essential if you want to keep safe and prevent further accidents should components or frames fail.

Tools required:
· **M6 and M5 taps and tapping wrench**
· **cutting paste**
· **cleaning kit, including rags and degreaser/spray lube**
· **frame alignment tool**
· **rear dropout alignment tool**
· **rear derailleur alignment tool**
· **string**
· **ruler**
· **Vernier calipers**

1 The Park frame alignment tool used here makes alignment assessment easier. The tool rests on the head tube and seat tube, and the pointer gauge is adjusted to sit on the outside of the dropout. The gauge is then set and flipped over to the other side. If the bike is symmetrical, the gauge will not have to be readjusted.

2 Another simple way to check alignment is to ride the bike with no hands, but please don't try this if you aren't confident. If the bike wants to turn without your assistance, this usually means there is a tracking problem. For a far safer quick check, you just need a long piece of string. Wrap it around the head tube and trap either end under the quick-release skewer, or get someone to hold it, while you measure the string. The string needs to be very taut. We have removed the wheel for clarity but it should be in place for an accurate reading.

3 On a full suspension bike, it can be easier to use the string technique rather than the alignment gauge; the shock and pivots often stick out at the seat tube so there is no place for the alignment tool to rest. Interrupted seat tubes can also create problems. But whatever frame you have, the principle remains the same: the head and seat tubes must align with the rear dropouts.

4 The critical measurement will be between the seat tube and either side of the length of string. A difference of 1–2 mm is acceptable and won't affect the bike's handling. However, if you have crashed and the measurement is more than 4–5mm, the frame may require attention from either a qualified frame builder or the manufacturer.

5 Rear dropouts on mountain bikes are usually made from large chunks of aluminum and as such are very unlikely to bend. The dropout alignment tools shown here are used to check that the rear end is correctly spaced and aligned for the rear wheel. With the dropout tools fully inserted in the drop out, the central sections can be adjusted to meet in the middle. If they don't meet up, the dropouts have been twisted. These tools are long so that the mechanic can 'cold set' (bend) them slightly to meet perfectly.

6 It is essential to face the bottom bracket shell and the head tube. This has already been explained in the headsets and bottom bracket sections (see pages 123–29 and 149–53), but it's important to remember that if you don't have these tools, the bike shop should prepare the frame for you.

7 Getting the right bottom bracket is essential too. Measure across the bottom bracket faces and install the appropriate unit, which will be either 73 mm or 68 mm. Fitting the wrong size will alter the chainline and mess up your shifting. See pages 149–53 for more on bottom brackets.

8 Water bottle bosses get clogged up with paint and, on steel frames, can rust up. Aluminum frames have riveted bottle bosses, which can be replaced with a specialist tool. Tap out the threads before you attach a bottle cage with an M5 tap. Be careful not to go too far. You will need the same size tool for rack fittings and cable guides as well, so it's worth buying one.

9 Cantilever studs can also rust up. Tapping the threads will ensure that the bolts secure the brake firmly and that the bolt will not be crossthreaded as you tighten it. On good frames the studs are replaceable and it's worth replacing them every year or so as they do wear and make the brakes rattle around. If you have excessive brake squeal, new studs can be the solution.

10 The rear derailleur hanger is possibly the most vulnerable part of the mountain bike frame. Many frames have replaceable hangers, which may require replacing after a serious crash. Simply unbolt the replaceable part and order a new one from your dealer. However, if you have dropped your bike, there may be a slight bend in the hangers. This can play havoc with your gear shift. The rear derailleur alignment tool used here allows you to check and cold set the gear hanger.

11 Once you have screwed the tool into the dropout, you can position it at several points around the wheel. The gauges on the tool allow you to lock it off using the wheel rim as a reference. If the gap between the gauges varies, you will have to adjust the dropout until there is a uniform gap all around.

12 Perfect shifting can only be achieved with a straight derailleur, so check this after every stack. If you have bent an aluminum dropout several times, you will need to replace it as it may snap. Once you have 'set' the hanger you can replace the rear derailleur.

13 Finally, remember to cover the frame at the points that rub on the cables and place a chainstay protector under the chain. These vulnerable positions will wear through the paint in no time, usually on the first ride. Neoprene protectors are a good idea as the chain literally bounces off them.

TIPS

- Rust is the first step on the road to frame failure. Corrosion shows that parts and frames are weakened, so clean off and treat rust as soon as it develops. On frames this can be best done by a re-spraying service.
- On steel frames use Waxoil on the inside of the frame tubes to protect them from rust. This is a spray-on treatment and helps prevent rust forming on the inside of your frame. This stuff is used on car chassis and tubes that are left outside.
- Get together with some riding buddies and all buy one expensive frame tool each. You can then share around the bigger work shop tools when you need them.
- Titanium doesn't rust. It's also really tough, so it will blunt taps and threading frame tools. Be careful when buying a titanium bike and make sure the frame comes pre-prepared – many bike shops will refuse to reface and tap titanium bottom brackets as it blunts expensive cutters.
- Full suspension bikes need to be in track, but often any misalignment will be just pivot wear and tear. Replace pivot bushes regularly and check that the bolts are tightened to the recommended torque. Always follow the manufacturer's recommendations. See pages 130–34 for more on suspension setup.

Dropout width

Measure across the dropouts between the inner faces. Mountain bike hubs are usually 135 mm. Road bikes (and very old mountain bike frames) are 130 mm. Singlespeed hubs and BMX hubs can be 110 mm, 115 mm or 120 mm. A narrower gap will make removing the wheels a little trickier, and over-wide dropouts can distort the rear end when you clamp up the quick-release lever.

Bottom bracket servicing and fitting

Bottom brackets are either square taper, ISIS, Octalink or 'through axle'. Most Shimano units are sealed and are designed to be thrown away when they wear out. However, with some more expensive brackets you can replace the bearings, in a similar way to cartridge-bearing hubs. If you have Shimano Hollowtech II cranks or a through axle, turn to pages 152–53 for specific information on these types.

Early mountain bike versions, which used loose ball bearing cup and cone composites that required attention even after the smallest rain fall, needed the patience of a bird watcher to set up without play or dragging. However, in recent years the one-piece unit with sealed bearings and a fiddle-free cartridge housing has been developed and can be set up to be smooth running and trouble free. Both types of unit thread into a bottom bracket shell in the frame, with the right-hand cup threading in counter-clockwise (as it is a left-hand thread) and the left-hand cup threading in clockwise (as it is a standard right-hand thread).

Square taper

On a square-taper bottom bracket, a two-degree angled taper is machined on four faces of the axle to give you a tight precision fit in the square-tapered holes in the alloy cranks. This is a fairly standard engineering technique and gives a large contact area at the connection between the cranks and the axle. Check that the fit is correct for your crank when buying a new bottom bracket. The usual cause of creaking cranks is either dirt in this area or an incompatible fit.

Octalink and ISIS

Octalink and ISIS systems use a splined axle that is oversized and therefore less vulnerable to twisting forces than the standard square taper. They are also lighter. The central sleeve keeps the bearings sealed from water and dirt that can get in from the inside via the frame tubes, and also acts as an accurate spacer to hold the cups and bearings in the correct position. They are usually made from aluminum or plastic.

Lock rings are not always necessary in modern cassette-type brackets as they have a standard fit. Shimano uses a system that means the chainset is held in a preset position on the axle. This ensures perfect alignment of the drivetrain. Adjustable brackets are better for cranks that may require moving from side to side to attain the best position or chain line; they can then be set into position using the lock rings.

Bolts and threads

The bottom bracket axle has threads tapped into either end of it for accepting the crank bolts. The crank bolts are normally Allen key bolts in plastic washers (to cover the crank extractor threads), or captive bolt systems that enable the crank to be removed in the loosening action. The bottom bracket threads in most mountain bikes are 'English' pattern (marked 1.370" x 24 TPI).

Regardless of what type of system your bike has, failing to prepare the frame properly will mean that the bottom bracket unit will not sit properly in the bike. So it may spin around okay, but once the cranks and chain are installed a poorly fitted bottom bracket will damage the bearings and the unit will not run efficiently.

The tools needed to do this job are very expensive and require careful handling. This may mean you have to get a good bike shop to do the first few (cutting) steps of this sequence for you, but it is essential that the threads are cleaned and the faces squared up before you start.

Axle length

The axle length will depend on the type of crank you are using. Bottom bracket axles come in a range of lengths, from 103 mm to 124 mm. When you replace a unit, always use the same length axle. Shorter axles can mean that the chainrings rub on the frame, while longer ones will mess up your chain-line and your gears won't work. If you are fitting a new crank and bottom bracket, check with the manufacturer which length axle you will need to match your old setup.

Unusual crank setups will need special attention. For example, if you are fitting a chain device or a front derailleur that fits over the bottom bracket shell, apply plenty of anti-seize to these components before fitting. Measure the width of the bracket shell – it will be either 73 mm or 68 mm. Remove the plastic cable guide bolt from under the bottom bracket shell, as it will snag on the cutters when they run through the threads.

Tools required:
· **bottom bracket tool**
· **torque wrench**
· **quality thread cutters**
· **facing tool**
· **cutting paste**
· **cleaning fluid**
· **calipers or ruler (for measuring bottom bracket and shell)**
· **8 mm crank Allen key**
· **anti-seize compound or synthetic grease**
· **in-line tap set**

1 Tap the threads using a quality in-line tap set. Remember that the drive-side or right crank is a left-hand thread (tightens counter-clockwise) and the non-drive-side or left crank is a right-hand thread (tightens clockwise). The tool will have the thread type stamped onto the cutters for identification, but double-check that you have the right cutters before you use them. Turn the cutters gradually and evenly – don't force them in, they should cut easily. If they start to seize up, there may be an obstruction in the shell. Use plenty of cutting paste and keep turning until the cutters sit flush into the frame. This process cleans out any paint, rust and material from the shell and ensures that the threads are running parallel. This is important as the life of the bearings will be greatly improved if they sit square to the frame and to the cranks; they will also be noise free and easier to remove.

2 Once you have tapped the threads, you can face the right-hand edge of the bottom bracket. When you are using the facing tool, you will need plenty of cutting paste. Remember not to run the tool backward as this can damage the cutter. Keep a close eye on the bracket face and check that it is clear of paint and completely square (it should look smooth and shiny all over).

3 Clean out the frame's bottom bracket shell thoroughly with a degreaser and dry it off. Then dress all the threads with plenty of anti-seize or quality synthetic grease. The bottom bracket is often neglected for many months, so how easy it is to remove the bottom bracket depends on how well it was prepared before it was put in.

4 The new unit will have one removable side, which is usually on the non-drive side. Pull this off so that the unit can be installed into the drive side first. This side has a left-hand thread and tightens counter-clockwise. If the threads have been properly prepared, you will be able to turn the unit with your fingers. Spin it in until there is about 1 cm of thread left. You will now be able to insert the non-drive-side cup. This tightens clockwise and will mesh with the cartridge inside the shell. Most Shimano brackets have a taper on the inside that allows them to self-locate. Again, tighten this with your fingers until there is about 1 cm of thread left showing.

5 Make sure that the bracket is tight in the frame. This requires special tools and quite a bit of leverage. Shimano brackets use a special tool that sits in serrations around the edge of the cup. Most other brackets use a set of holes that accept a pin wrench or peg tool and a lock ring to hold it in position. If you don't get the right tools for the bracket, you risk making a mess of the unit and your frame. Next, use the bottom bracket tool to tighten the unit into the frame. Make sure that the shoulder of the unit on the drive side is tight up against the frame first. This is to make sure that the chainset will sit in the right place and that it will not loosen off. Once the drive side is tight you can tighten the non-drive side. Tighten both cups to 40–50 Nm.

6 Clean up any excess grease around the frame and threads, then reinstall the cranks. Replace the cable guide, being aware that the bolt may need shortening if you have fitted a different type of bracket. Do not tighten this bolt into the outside of the unit as it can damage the seal. See pages 155–57 for more on removing and installing cranks.

PRO WORKSHOP TIPS

- If you ruin or cross-thread the threads in your bottom bracket, you can have it reamed and rethreaded to a larger size. Some bikes (mainly Italian road bikes) have 'Italian' threads (marked: 36 x 24"), which are slightly larger than the usual English brackets and can save you chucking an otherwise good frame. Most good bike shops will be able to do this for you.
- Titanium frames will have been properly prepared at the factory. Few cutters are capable of cutting titanium easily and you will blunt a steel cutter very quickly if you try – titanium is very tough stuff. Also, when assembling any threaded titanium components, remember to use copper slip (Ti Prep) as it will prevent materials from seizing completely. If a titanium frame needs facing, take it to a specialist frame builder who will have the right tools.

Integrated bottom bracket servicing

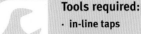

Tools required:
- **in-line taps**
- **facing tool**
   (Note: If you don't have a facing tool, you will need the bike shop to do some of the preparatory work for you. The bottom bracket has to be properly faced for it to work properly.)
- **Shimano C-spanner TL-FC32 (supplied with bottom bracket)**
- **Shimano axle-bolt tool TL-FC16 (supplied with bottom bracket)**
- **Allen keys**
- **torque wrench**
- **grease (Shimano Anti-Seize is good)**

The Shimano Hollowtech II Crank setup is very easy to install and service. It takes its design influence from the headset – basically, it's an oversize tube secured at either end with the cranks, just like your forks are held in place with the stem. The system is known as a through-axle or integrated crank. The drive side will sit perfectly flush to the frame, so the chainline will be just right for Shimano drive systems (derailleurs, chains and cassettes). Chainrings are replaced in the same way as any crank.

The bearings in the bottom bracket unit are spaced farther apart and outside the frame's bottom bracket shell, allowing for a larger axle diameter and a much stiffer crankset than you would get on a square taper, an Octalink or an ISIS splined type. Many other crank manufacturers, including Bontrager, Truvativ, Race Face and DMR, have adopted this type of system for strength and reliability. The result is better functionality for one of the weakest points of a bike's drivetrain.

Important note

All frames must be properly prepared before you attempt to fit a bottom bracket. Bearings and cups must run parallel and threads must allow you to fit the bracket without forcing it with a tool. Cross-threading bottom brackets can be a costly mistake, so if you are in doubt get an experienced mechanic to prepare and fit the bracket for you – ask to watch them do it and you'll learn for next time.

1 Face the bracket shell on both sides. This *must* be done before the bearing unit can be set up properly. Because the bearings are placed on the outside of the frame's bottom bracket shell and they have to be parallel, you need a flat, very clean bracket. You will find that some frames need more preparation than others. Clean out any metal shavings and particles from the bottom bracket and use some Shimano anti-seize grease on the threads.

2 Spacers are needed and are placed on the drive side. This ensures the correct spacing and correct chainline is maintained for efficient shifting. Measure the width of the bottom bracket shell – it will be either 68 mm or 73 mm. The number of spacers needed depends on the width of the bottom bracket: three spacers are required for a 68 mm bottom bracket shell (one on the left-hand cup); two spacers are required for a 68 mm bottom bracket shell and bracket-type front derailleur (one on either side); one spacer is required for a 73 mm bottom bracket shell (on the right-hand side); no spacers are required for a 73 mm bottom bracket shell and bracket-type fitting front derailleur.

3 Fit the internal plastic cover to the right (drive) side cup and thread it into the bottom bracket shell. Once again, remember that the drive side is a left-hand thread (turns counter-clockwise) and the non-drive side is a right-hand thread (turns clockwise). At this stage, do not tighten the cups completely, just finger-tighten both cups into place.

4 It's best to locate the left side cup (right-hand thread – clockwise) before you tighten the right side cup completely, as the plastic sleeve has to mate with both cups inside the bottom bracket shell. Once they are both flush with the edge of the bottom bracket, tighten them to 35–50 Nm using the C-spanner, which is usually supplied with the unit.

5 The right-hand crank and bottom bracket axle are fixed as a 'one-piece' complete unit. Push the axle into the bottom bracket cups all the way – there is no need to force this on, a gentle tap with the flat of your hand will make sure it is in the right position. There is a flat surface on the inside of the crank that has to sit flush with the outside face of the bearing, so make sure that you can't see a gap between the crank and the bottom bracket bearing face.

6 There are two rubber O-rings that fit over the crank axle to seal the bearing units. One has to be installed on the drive side, the other before the left hand crank is added. Wet these seals with some grease so they slip over the axle easily.

7 There are two flat sections on the splined axle, which self-locate into the crank so that the cranks line up perfectly. The crank won't go on any other way, so don't try to force it. Push the crank on the axle and place a hand on each crank and push them firmly together. This will check that they are both seated correctly with the cranks tight up against the bearing cups.

8 There is a cap to thread into the open end of the left-hand crank axle and, in the same way that the headset cap works (see pages 124–25), this cap tightens the two cranks onto the bearings. The cap only needs to be 'finger tight' to take up the play, but there is a special Shimano or Park tool to help tighten this cap.

9 Lastly, tighten the two Allen bolts on the left hand crank arm evenly; do them up alternately and a little at a time until you reach the recommended tightening torque of 10–15 Nm. The cranks should spin freely, so if there are tight spots or wobbles you have done something wrong.

10 Removing the crankset is simple. It requires no special crank pullers or wrenches – just undo the fixing bolts and the cap and pull the left-hand crank off. However, if you do remove the unit make sure that you follow steps 7–9 in order to reinstall it correctly.

Standard cranks and chainrings

Chainsets or cranksets are the engine room of the bike – that is, the bit that gets all the power directly from your legs and helps you rip up the trail. They consist of three main components: the crank, the chainrings and the spider.

Q factor

This is the distance across the pedal faces, i.e. how wide your legs are apart. This should be approximately 160 mm for mountain bikes and 145 mm for road bikes. You can't go much narrower or the cranks hit the chainstays. A wide Q factor is bad because all your joints have to compensate; your knees get especially abused and bend the wrong way with a wide Q factor.

A short bottom bracket is stiffer and lighter. You also get good ankle clearance with a short bottom bracket and a low-profile crank. A 122 mm bottom bracket is always going to give you a bigger Q factor and also a more flexible power transfer.

Crank arms

The crank arm has to be really stiff – this is an absolute priority. Stamping and pulling on a strong crank relays all the power you can muster to the rear wheel, while flexible cranks are inefficient and are more likely to break unexpectedly. Their shape should be smooth and flowing, and there should be no sudden changes in shape or section. Sharp pockets and cut-out areas cause stress raisers and cracks to start, leading to eventual breaks.

Crank arms are usually either 170 mm or 175 mm long. The one you use is up to you – there are no set rules – but will also be governed very slightly by your leg length. 175 mm cranks give better leverage but aren't ideal for riders shorter than 5'6". Most manufacturers will put 170 mm crank arms on 16 inch bikes for this reason.

Triple through-axle or integrated crank

The Shimano through-axle-style integrated cranks are so simple it's a wonder no-one thought of it before (yes, there have been a few similar systems, but Shimano always seems to get it right). The tubular axle and oversized external bearings make for a very strong pedaling platform. Servicing this style of crank doesn't require any complicated tools and they can be adjusted with an Allen key. However, they should be installed correctly.

Chainrings

Chainrings come in hundreds of sizes and are made in a variety of manufacturing processes: stamped, CNC-machined and sometimes part-cut, part-machined. The current trend is for ramps and rivets to assist the chain in shifting. The usual Shimano drive setup will be 32–22-toothed rings, but any number of combinations are possible on most cranks. There are several bolt patterns readily available: old-style Shimano compact drive, micro drive and so on. Make sure that whichever type you use has the right PCD (Pitch Circle Diameter) chainring for your crank.

Chainring bolts

Chainring bolts are made from steel, titanium or aluminum, depending on your pocket. Steel bolts are probably the best as they are cheap and strong. They need greasing every now and then as they can seize if left to rust. Use copper grease on the bolts. Titanium bolts are very light but very expensive, and also require special attention if left for long periods of time as they can seize up. Use plenty of copper slip or anti-grease compound on them and only tighten to the manufacturer's recommended torque setting. Aluminum bolts are really light but not very strong and can snap off. Chainring bolts take a 5 mm Allen key and should be tightened gradually and in sequence (that is, not from left to right but from opposite bolt to opposite bolt) so that you don't overtighten them and to ensure that the rings run true. There is one set for the two large chainwheels and one set for the granny ring.

Spider

Spiders can be part of the same four- or five-arm forging in cheaper cranks or as a separate bolt-on section that can be replaced if need be. Most manufacturers have taken this a bit further by making the big ring a part of the spider and attaching the middle and the granny rings with four bolts rather than five. This means that you can retrofit the standard five-point fixing rings. Flexible spiders allow the chainrings to move when the front derailleur tries to shift, giving you sloppy shifts, and bent or out-of-line spiders will make the gears rough and upset the shifting.

Removing cranks

Removing cranks is simple as long as you use the right tools; and replacing cartridge bottom brackets couldn't be easier, so if you're still running a cup and loose ball-bearing bracket, you should think about changing soon. A lot of bottom brackets are 'fit and forget' units (i.e., once it's in you don't need to worry about it), but some of them are very expensive and a bit too much for most pockets.

Tools required:
- Allen keys
- crank puller and wrench
- torque wrench and 8 mm Allen socket
- copper slip
- chainline tool
- lock ring tools
- vise or large wrench

1 On standard cranks, the fixing bolt has an 8 mm Allen head with the washer as an integral part of the bolt. The black plastic washer pictured here acts as a dust cover to keep dirt out of the threads. Old-style cranks still use a 14 or 15 mm hex-headed bolt and washer protected by a separate dust cap.

2 Once you have removed the bolts and washers, remove the crank using a crank puller. This tool is essential for taking the cranks off the bike, and good ones won't damage the threads or the end of the axle. Clean out any mud from the crank threads with a squirt of spray lube. Thread the crank puller into the crank as far as it will go, then undo the center bolt first so it fits as flush as possible, being careful to get it in straight. Note: ISIS and Octalink cranks require a larger head on the crank pulling tool.

3 Once you have correctly inserted the puller, tighten the arm (or central bolt) towards the bottom bracket axle. The arm rests on the end of the axle and the pushing/pulling motion forces the crank off the square axle taper. The crank will then drop off on the floor, so be careful to keep hold of it. Note: If you only insert the crank puller in by a few threads, or cross-thread it, it will strip out the threads when you tighten the center bolt to pull off the crank. Once the threads are stripped your crank will be useless.

4 Always retighten cranks to the recommended torque setting and check them after the first ride as they can loosen slightly due to the pedaling force.

5 ISIS axles have a symmetrical splined pattern on the axle and it's worth cleaning this every time you remove the crank arms. Shimano Octalink cranks are very different so don't try to mix them up.

6 The chainline tool assesses the correct spacing of the bottom bracket axle and the alignment of the cassette sprockets with the chainrings. Basically, there should be a straight line between the middle chainring and the middle sprocket of the cassette.

7 For ideal shifting you really want the chain to be at its straightest in the middle chainring and in the middle of the cassette, allowing for optimum spread of gears with less chain angle. This improves shifting, prolongs the life of the chain and prevents it from coming off unexpectedly.

8 Fitting chainrings is very simple, but make sure that you get the correct size for your crank. Use a decent copper slip on the bolts and bolt holes. Not only does this prevent the bolts from seizing, but it also stops them 'drying out' and creaking as time goes by.

9 Chainring bolts can rotate in the crank so use a bolt wrench to hold the nut at the back to prevent it from spinning.

10 The spider is the central yoke that attaches the rings to the cranks. It's probably the most important area of the setup for two very important reasons: first, it's responsible for the accurate alignment of the rings to the rear cassette (chainline) and second, it needs to be super stiff and totally flex free. Most spiders can be removed from the crank and replaced if they are bent or twisted. The DMR Chieftain crank shown here has a split ring on the inside of the lock ring to prevent it from loosening.

11 Use this Shimano lock ring tool to remove the lock ring. This is the industry standard for most crank spider lock rings. Hold the tool in a vise or use a large wrench.

12 Lock rings are usually factory fitted and therefore very tight, so be careful not to slip. Some Race Face cranks have replaceable spider arm ends and Shimano cranks all bolt to one chainring. However, you do need to know how to replace the chainrings and spider should you crash into a log and bend the whole lot.

FURTHER INFORMATION

Web sites

Most manufacturers' Web sites have all the information you'll need, but here are a few from my bookmarks list:

www.parktool.com
An excellent resource for all tool and spare parts reference information. Also good for torque setting references and how to use Park tools.

www.shimano.com
Provides information on spares and product availability and regular technical updates.

www.sheldonbrown.com
This is one of the most popular and informative sites for bike-related problems. Quirky, but always up to date.

www.dtswiss.com
A useful reference site for wheelbuilders. Provides a spoke length calculator and a wheel weight calculator.

www.bikemagic.com
A consumer site with useful technical features and product reviews. Includes all the latest gear and gadgets.

www.weightweenies.com
Great if you're into building the lightest bike possible.

www.cyclingnews.com
News and technical features for mountain and road bikes alike.

www.finishline.com
The top lube company. Includes some interesting stuff for home mechanics.

www.sram.com
Provides information for those running SRAM components.

Books

Further reading for budding professional mechanics includes:

Sutherlands Repair Manual

Barnetts Bicycle Repair Manual

Shimano Spare Parts by Shimano

The Bicycle Wheel by Jobst Brandt (Avocet Inc., 1993)

The Art of Wheel Building by Gerd Schraner (Ann Arbor Press, 1999)

GLOSSARY

Items in italics denote another glossary entry.

32-hole: hubs and rims come in various drillings: 32-hole is the one most commonly used on mountain bikes, but I've also seen 28- and 36-hole used occasionally. 36-holed wheels will be slightly stronger, but slightly heavier; 28-holed ones will be lighter but weaker. You should relate the amount of spokes to your body weight – for example, heavier riders (above 185 pounds) might be better off with 36-holed wheels, whereas smaller riders (under 140 pounds) could get away with 28-holed ones.

4130: a certain grade of cromoly steel tubing. 4130 is used a lot in the bike business because it's light, strong and easy to work with.

6061 aluminum: pure aluminum alloyed with magnesium and silicon, this needs to be artificially aged and heat-treated to return the metal to its T6 strength after welding.

7000-series aluminum: this denotes that the main alloying agent in the aluminum is zinc, whereas *6061 aluminum* has primary alloying agents of magnesium and silicon.

7005 aluminum: another type of aluminum, usually heat-treated.

Active suspension: in simple terms, this means that the suspension will work independently of pedaling or braking forces.

Aheadset: a system of clamping the handlebar stem to the fork steerer without needing an internal expanding fixing, pioneered by Dia-Compe. This saves weight and is easier to maintain and adjust.

Air/oil: a suspension system that relies on air for the spring and oil for the damping control. The advantage over coiled springs is its light weight.

Anti-suck plate: prevents the chains from being drawn into the chainrings (see *chain suck*).

Bar end: designed to provide an alternative climbing position, enabling easier out-of-the-saddle 'pumping' of the bars.

BMX: short for Bicycle Motocross. BMX bikes are small-wheeled race bikes designed for closed circuits that are good for stunts, handle quickly and have no gears.

Bottom bracket: the central axle of the cranks.

Braze-ons: anything that is attached to the frame that allows you to add components like cables, bottle cages, racks or gear mechanisms.

Bushing: a bearing part that has no balls or rollers in it. Suspension systems rely on them for sliders and pivots (usually made from nylon).

Butting/butted: a process used on steel, titanium or aluminum tubes whereby the ends are drawn thicker for strength at stress or weld points. The middles of the tubes can be made thinner and therefore lighter as they are under less stress. Tubes can be single-, double-, triple- or even quad-butted. Butting/butted also refers to spokes.

Cassette: the cassette cluster is now the accepted industry standard attachment for rear sprockets. The rings slot onto the cassette and are locked on with a threaded lock ring. In the old days, the freewheel (the bit that clicks) was part of the sprocket setup, which screwed onto a threaded part of the hub. Cassette hubs allow the bearings to be placed farther apart, strengthening the axle considerably.

Cantilever brake: a lightweight and super-powerful rim brake that allows quick and responsive braking. An age-old design, it relies on a simple pivot point and levers to give it effortless action.

Center to center: the measurement from the center of the crank axle to the center of the top tube is the usual way of measuring a frame. Mountain bikes are measured in inches, road bikes in centimeters.

Chainline: the ideal chainline is when the chain is parallel to the center line of the bike, which passes from the center of the rear hub to the center of the bottom bracket when the chain is on the middle ring at the front and around the center of the rear sprockets. To achieve the correct chainline, you have to have the correct bottom bracket axle length.

Chainslap: the annoying sound of the chain tap-dancing on your chainstay paintwork, usually heard when traveling at speed or out of control over rough ground.

Chain suck: the result of worn chainrings – the chain remains stuck to the 'back-side' of the chainring and becomes lodged in the frame and crank. This can damage the paintwork and stop you dead.

Coil/oil: a suspension system that relies on a metal spring for shock absorption. The spring rate can be altered on a coil/oil system, and they are far more reliable and robust than an *air/oil* system. However, they are heavier.

Compact drive: a Shimano invention designed to save weight and improve chainring grounding clearance. Compact drives adopt 42/32/22 chainrings, as opposed to the more traditional 26/36/46 (the successor to Suntour's Microdrive setup from around 1993). The smaller chainrings are complemented by a larger cassette ratio with an 11-tooth top sprocket, but some people find they run out of gears, normally known as 'spinning out'.

Compatibility: before index shifting, there was a period in mountain bike history when everything worked with everything else – not very well, but at least most manufacturers' shifters, *derailleurs,* chains and freewheels worked happily with one another, albeit a little basically. Then along came index shifting and everybody went in all sorts of different directions – and the compatibility nightmare began.

Derailleur: a French invention, perfected by Shimano, which shifts the chain across the chainrings and sprockets. Also known as a 'mech'.

Disc brakes: the braking system fast becoming the choice of all mountain bikers. Originally heavy and unreliable, they are now very light and well made.

Elastomers: chunks or cylinders of special high-density plastic that have elastic properties and, in their suspension fork form, are very light. They have a tendency to rebound more quickly than an oil-damped fork, so they can 'pogo' about at times, but are much easier to service.

Eyeletted rims: eyelets are used around the rim drillings to spread the nipple tension and build a stronger wheel.

Fillet: extra metal that is applied to the weld area to both strengthen the weld and provide a smoother finish, which is achieved by hand-filing the entire weld.

Flat bar: the traditional cross-country shaped bar, with a three-degree sweep. Usually used with *bar ends*.

Flatties: pedals with a large platform. Used by dirt jumpers, trials riders and downhillers, they offer more control for riders who do less pedaling and more 'riding'.

Forging/forged: a manufacturing process that usually involves heat and impact to 'force' metal into complicated, yet strong, shapes.

Frame: the central and main component of the bike.

Geometry: fitting suspension forks to a *hardtail* alters the frame angles because the longer suspension forks lift the front of the bike slightly. Bike companies have various ways to rectify the problem. The easiest (and cheapest) way is to make a longer than normal rigid fork in the first place so that when the bouncy fork is fitted it doesn't affect the handling. This creates a small problem, however, in that you have to design the rest of the frame around this long rigid fork in the first place. Reputable bike companies do this by crimping the top tube, lowering the head tube and steepening the frame angles.

Granny gear: the smallest chainring (usually 22- or 24-tooth) – suitable for grannies to get up hills, presumably!

Gripshift: lightweight twist shifter made by American component company SRAM. This unit is very simple yet effective, due to a small number of moving parts.

Gussett: added reinforcement for frames, especially important around the head tube where *fillets* of material are attached to prevent damage.

Hardtail: a bike with a rigid frame, usually for cross-country riding. Many jump bikes are now hardtails because of their increased maneuverability.

Head/seat angle: a steeper head angle has the effect of quickening and sharpening the steering by moving the forks further towards the down tube, making the steering more direct.

Headsets: headsets come in three sizes: 1 inch, $1\frac{1}{8}$ inch and 1.5 inch. All are still commonly used on mountain bikes, although the middle size ($1\frac{1}{8}$ inch) is the most common.

Hubs: these are sealed and run on either cartridge or ball bearings.

Low-profile cranks: low-profile cranks keep the chainrings and center of the crank spider closer to the *bottom bracket* shell. This enables a better *chainline*, as the cranks are shaped to give chainstay clearance.

Lugs: the traditional joining parts of a steel-frame tube.

Machined rims: rims are made from a strip of alloy, so have to be joined to form a circle. If the join isn't perfectly flush, it can be a rough spot where the brake blocks stick. Machining the rim scrapes it so it's perfectly flush all the way around, and also gets rid of any anodizing, which, unlike alloy, is not a good surface to brake on.

MCU: micro-cellular urethane is basically a type of *elastomer* with extra bounce and durability. MCU is most popular in modern fork technology (like Rock Shox Judys and Manitou Mach 5s) and are light and easily replaced.

Monocoque: a method of hollow tube construction. Bike companies use monocoques because they are lighter than conventional tubes, and they can manipulate the wall thickness to achieve certain ride characteristics.

Ovalized tubing: ovalizing a tube where it joins with another tube can help it resist specific forces by increasing the relevant contact area. At the *bottom bracket*, ovalizing helps to resist the side-to-side forces caused by stamping on the pedals, while at the head tube it can be used to resist the twisting forces caused by wrestling with the bars.

PCD: pitch circle diameter – the distance between the fixing bolts on chainrings.

Pivot point: where the suspension lever pivots. The farther forward the pivot point, the plusher the suspension will be in the saddle (and firmer out of it). When the rider is seated there is greater leverage on the pivot point and hence the shock. As the rider stands the weight moves forward, thereby lessening the leverage and unweighting the shock.

Plain-gauge tubes: tubes that are the same thickness all the way through, as opposed to *butted* tubes, which are thicker at the ends than in the center. Butted tubing is lighter and more resilient, but also more expensive to make than plain-gauge tubing, which is one of the reasons you only see it on top-end aluminum bikes.

Quill stems: these are used with standard headsets on threaded fork columns (or steerers) and used to be the norm on mountain bikes. However, they are very rare these days as the threadless headset clamp-on stem system has taken over. Quill-style stems tighten up with a long Allen bolt that drives an internal or sliding wedge out, literally jamming it into the fork steerer tube. This system is simpler and more height-adjustable than its more modern brother but slightly heavier and not as strong.

Rapidfire: a Shimano invention from c. 1990; found on XT groupsets at first, it has been perfected over the years.

Rapid-rise: the reverse shifting *derailleur*.

Replaceable rear dropout: these are important on carbon or aluminum bikes since the rear *derailleur* hanger is impossible to weld back on if it snaps in a crash.

Rigid forks: rigid forks, although a little archaic, still have a lot going for them. They don't move or flex when cornering (affecting control) and they don't bob up and down on the climbs (robbing the rider of energy). Popular with trials riders.

Riser bars: provide a higher position and more control than a *flat bar*.

Sag: the amount the suspension compresses as you simply sit on the bike.

Shimano XT: next in line to *Shimano XTR* groupset from component giant Shimano.

Shimano XTR: top-of-the range groupset from component giant Shimano.

Singletrack: a track that is just wide enough for one bike, often tight and twisting through woods or dense vegetation. Great fun!

Sliders: the part of the suspension fork that moves, usually anodized or plated so that it can move freely with less *stiction*.

Snakebites: a puncture caused by mashing into a sharp object at speed, squashing the inner tube between the object and the edge of the rim. Snakebite punctures are the curse of downhillers as they often happen when you least expect them to and the wheel can flat a while after the impact itself.

SPD: a Shimano abbreviation for their very own clipless off-road pedal that stands for Shimano Pedaling Dynamics. Referred to as 'spuds'. They enable quick, consistent positioning of your feet on the pedal, holding them firmly by use of a small metal cleat that snaps into either side of the double-sided pedal and are disengaged by simply twisting the foot outward.

Spider: the part of the crank that attaches the chainrings to the cranks.

Stanchion: the main part of the suspension fork – the part in which the sliders move up and down.

Steel frame: there's nothing like the feel of a steel frame – strong, light, easy to make and the friend of all mountain bikers. A steel frame is the real deal. Steel-framed bikes offer long life and a comfortable ride.

Stiction: like 'friction', but in suspension it is the effort required to move the shock.

Suspension-corrected geometry: most *hardtail* frames are now suitable for 100–120 mm forks. Older frames (pre-2000) may not be suitable as they have more 'relaxed' *geometry*.

Swaging: the process of squeezing and shaping the tube along its length, either to make the tube easier to weld and/or to distribute stress.

Thumb shifter: the first style of gear shift for mountain bikes, initially developed by Suntour, improved by Shimano and then copied by just about everyone else. The originals had ratchets inside to assist in the gearshift and used a friction gear mechanism – long before the introduction of index shifting. Indexed systems quickly moved the design on.

Toeclips and straps: when mountain biking was in its infancy, we all wore sneakers and used enormous bear-trap pedals. These were first used in conjunction with roadie-type clips and leather straps, which eventually gave way to plastic and nylon. Then came the SPD pedal, and clipless pedals are now pretty much the norm. The straps are very useful for holding things down, attaching bikes to roof-racks and so on.

Top-out: a knocking caused by the suspension returning too quickly, the most common reason being too much preload on the shock. 'Bottom out' is when you use all the travel up quickly and flat out the suspension.

Tubeless tires: a great invention for mountain biking. Because there is no tube, you are less likely to get *snakebite punctures*. You can run a lower tire pressure and therefore you get more traction and grip.

Weight: most mountain bikes weigh around the 25–27 pound mark. This would give you a pretty reasonable bike. If your bike weighs under 25 pounds, you're talking svelte. But as with anything, you pay for a low weight – lightweight parts, wheels, tires and exotic frame materials mean a hefty price tag. The more money you spend, the more weight you will save and the lighter your bike.

INDEX